DAMAGED GOODS

HEALING & DELIVERANCE FOR MARRIAGES

AUTHOR
SHAWNEY L. TIM

Copyright © 2020 by Shawney L. Tim and Wisdom in Print Publishing Company, Inc.

All rights reserved. No part of this book may be reproduced or transmitted in any form or by any means without written permission from the author.

All scriptures are taken from the King James Version of the Bible, unless otherwise stated.

Published by Wisdom in Print Publishing Company, Dr. Laytecia McKinney. www.iamwowmentor.com

ISBN 978-1-7357779-0-0

Printed in the United States of America

~DEDICATION~

I dedicate this book to my angel, my grandmother, the late Emma Mae Wingfield and my mother, Diane Wingfield.

Granny, I miss you. I can still hear your voice sometimes. Thank you for giving me the best childhood you could. Your strictness saved me (I see that now).

Mommy, (my Lady Bug), thank you for allowing God to change us both and become each other's rock. I love you beyond words!

TABLE OF CONTENTS

Foreword..v

Acknowledgments....................................vi

Introduction..viii

Chapter 1 Understanding the Power of Covenant   1

Chapter 2 Healing the Wounds Within   24

Chapter 3 Root Up, Tear Down and Destroy to Rebuild   53

Chapter 4 The False Perception of Marriage   72

Chapter 5 Family Secrets, the Silent Killer   86

Chapter 6 Forgiving the Unforgivable   99

Chapter 7 Is There Anything Too Hard for God   124

Dr. Laytecia Brooks-McKinney

~Foreword~

MANY DAUGHTERS HAVE DONE VIRTUOUSLY, BUT THOU EXCELLEST THEM ALL *(Proverbs 31:29)*.

It was by divine will that God placed Shawney L. Tim in my path of life. Shawney is gifted to write and release healing to the Nations through her wisdom and past experiences. She is indeed an overcomer, bold enough to tell her story to set captives free. I thank God for her relevancy and loving heart to want to help heal marriages.

As you read through the pages of this book, the words will come alive and your mouth will even drop open at times at her rawness and candid TRUTHS!

It was a great joy to publish her first of many books! "Damaged Goods", will serve as a blueprint to help heal, strengthen and restore the covenant of holy matrimony. Shawney explains the power of forgiveness between man and wife and God and man(woman) in such a captivating way that will open up your heart to be FREE of anything holding you hostage!

Dr. Laytecia McKinney
Senior Pastor | Author | Mentor | Publisher
www.iamwowmentor.com

~ACKNOWLEDGEMENTS~

To Abba, my Heavenly Father, thank you for placing me in my mother's womb. Thank you for choosing me for such a time as this. Thank you for all the downloads you gave me for this assignment. There is no way I could have done this without you sending angels and the Holy Spirit to assist me. Thank you for sending me to the Center for Manifestation and giving me two of the best earthly spiritual parents, Dr. Mark T. Jones and Prophetess Lisa Jones. Apostle Mark, your leadership has birthed me and pushed me into this new place in God and I am profoundly grateful. Prophetess Lisa, thank you for your prayers and being there every time, I call or need your words of wisdom. I love you both to life!

To Annette Feazell, thank you for igniting the fire in me to write. I never thought I could until I sat in your class and your words pierced my heart. Sonya Cebella, thank you so much for holding me accountable to this assignment; all your texts gave me the push I needed to not give up and complete the assignment. My frienny-friend-friend, Nicole Williams, thank you for being you…that friend to read my book and give me your honest feedback; I thank God for our friendship.

My book mentor Dr. Laytecia McKinney, you are heaven sent. As a first-time writer I had no idea how to do this. I just began to write and waited for God to send you to help push this baby out. Your wisdom and words of encouragement were the wings I needed to fly. Much love and respect I have for you.

To my favorite and only biological daughter, Ms. Dacia De'Caria Carter, I love you so much! Thank you for pushing me to tell it all and to be transparent. Well I could not tell it ALL in one book so there will be a Part 2. When I wanted to take certain things out you would say "NO leave it in there." My true break-through came when you used our story for one of your productions, "When God is in It." You pushed me to write and direct the production, birthing forth a new passion in me. Thank you for choosing me to be your mother. I remember being so mad at you when you got pregnant but thank you for giving me one of my greatest gifts, Jada Heavenly. She is joy and laughter for my heart. I love you both Infinity!

Finally, there could be no damaged goods without the love to my love story. Reggie Tim Jr., what a journey! I do not know what you saw in my crazy self almost 28 years ago, on Main Street. Thank you for seeing pass all the crazy and making me laugh. To see the work, we put in and what God has done in and through our marriage, makes my heart smile. You have pushed me beyond what I thought was my capacity to love and forgive anyone. As God continues to restore, heal, and deliver our marriage, I pray we will remain one and faithful to the call, and continue to go from glory to glory. I will always be your Dook and you will always be my Babe! Forever yours!

Shawney

~INTRODUCTION~

"Damaged Goods" is a guide to true healing and deliverance for marriages told through the real testimony of my life and marriage. I never imagined my mess becoming a miracle. I never imagined my husband and I being called by God to bring forth correction, healing, and deliverance for others through our story because it is not a pretty story. Our story is not wrapped up in a big pretty box with a pretty bow tied on the top. Our story is the complete opposite and totally outside of the box.

When the Holy Spirit told me to write this book I did not understand why. Why share my most painful experiences with the world? Why subject my marriage to the warfare I knew would come with me saying yes to this assignment? Why me? Why us? With all the questions I had, I only received a one answer response…PURPOSE! It was not about the why, it was about the what. What God was doing and reestablishing in the earth realm, the purpose and order of martial covenant.

I am so honored that you have decided to take this journey with me as I open up and let you into some places I have never shared or only shared with a select few. I ask that you prepare yourself for some real transparency, biblical truths, and revelation. As you take this journey with me, keep an open heart and open mind. I will go some places religion has not gone. Journal your thoughts, pray the prayers out loud (everyday if you have to), believe God to heal and restore not just your marriage but every marriage that is going through infidelity, financial instability, false perception, past hurts, spiritual wounds, loving the unlovable, and forgiving the unforgivable.

I thank God for choosing me for this assignment and may your damaged goods become a beautiful love story.

Chapter One

UNDERSTANDING THE POWER OF COVENANT RELATIONSHIP

Cov-e-nant – "an agreement;" commitment; promise; a coming together, agreeing on promise; a lifelong friendship.

God is a God of covenant relationship; he honors covenant. Marriage is a covenant relationship between the man, woman, and God. Marriage is not just a legal binding on paper; it is a promise to God! I believe that the divorce rate is high, especially within the Body of Christ because we do not honor covenant, nor do we understand the power of covenant relationship. I do not understand how a man and woman must stand before God and a cloud of witnesses to be married and not have to do the same when getting divorced. God made promises to us centuries ago and despite everything we have done from generation to generation to dishonor, disobey, and rebel against His will, he has yet to break his promises to us. On the contrary, we make promises and break them so carelessly. My prayer is that by the end of this chapter, a seed will be planted so the next time you have the urge to break any covenant relationship (especially marriage) the Holy Spirit will convict you and you will remember this chapter.

Genesis – The Beginning

Me and Reggie's beginning was happenstance. We both grew up in West Tampa and knew the same circle of people, but our paths had never crossed. My grandmother was the "candy lady" in the West Tampa projects. She set up a mini store in the kitchen of our apartment, Ms. Emma had anything you could buy at the regular store for cheaper. It was a blessing and a curse for my sister, cousin, and I; you would not believe the hours we spent on the weekends rolling coins for my grandmother to make a bank deposit. We could not enjoy being outside playing without someone coming up to us to buy a pickle or something! We hated it! The blessing was that all those pennies, nickels, dimes, and quarters we rolled, rolled us up and out of the projects into a home. Reggie was on the other side of West Tampa, at the same time, being raised in a single parent home with his mom, sister, and cousin. His mom was a hardworking woman who would walk the streets of West Tampa to get to work, pay her bills, and take her children to school. It takes

Reggie to tell you the miles his mom put on his feet at such a young age. We grew up less than a mile from each other, yet our paths never crossed until 1991. We moved out of the projects around 1984, I went with my mom and step father to the south-east side of town called Claire Mel, while my grandmother, sister, and cousins moved into a home on the north side of town, far away from West Tampa.

    My uncle opened a small café in West Tampa, on Main Street, in 1991 and he needed help on the weekend, so I started working there. Main Street was the place to be on Friday and Saturday nights. The street would come alive! The smell of Barbeque King, the old-school kats at the Zanzibar, dressed in their Sunday's best, the line down the street to get in Club Boogie's, the dope boys showing off their cars with chrome rims, hydraulics, blasting their music to see whose bass was hitting the hardest, and lastly, the hot girls in their daisy dukes, biker shorts, and halter tops trying to get one of the dope boys to holla at them…Oh yes, it was on and popping! This particular Friday night was no different, except there was a tap on the order window, I opened the window and there he stood, "Lil Reggie." Our eyes met, and with a smirk on his face, he ordered fried gizzards and fries. Before I could close the window, he asked, "Hey what's your name?" I responded, "Shawney, what's your name?" He said, "They call me Lil Reggie. He said the food was nasty, but I could not tell because he kept coming back. I now know he was not coming back for the food; he was coming back for me. He would come to the window and spend hours talking to me and getting me in trouble with my uncle for talking too much and not working.

It did not take long before the long talks turned into an attraction and friendship; however, the courtship did not happen until three years later, when our paths crossed again in April 1994, at club "Celebrities." That night we exchanged phone numbers again and the next day the conversation picked up like we had never stopped talking. We were both in relationships, me living with my boyfriend and him living with his girlfriend. After weeks of talking, he asked me to go out to the movies with him. I agreed, only if he would go to church with me. We both snuck out for our first official date to the dollar movies to see "Above the Rim." Our second date was on a Sunday at St. John Progressive Missionary Baptist Church. I knew the only thing that could save a "dope boy" was Jesus! So, to church we went. Yes, I took the "dope boy" to church, not knowing God had a plan. I was wild, hot tempered, and a little crazy, but for some reason, Jesus was always a part of my craziness and if you wanted to be a part of my crazy world, you were going to need Jesus too.

Covenant Beginning

"In the beginning, God created the heaven and the earth. And the earth was without form, and void; and darkness was upon the face of the deep. And the Spirit of God moved upon the face of the waters. And God said, Let there be light; and there was light."
Genesis 1:1-3

COVENANT
An agreement, usually formal, between two or more persons to do or not do something specified.

Throughout the bible, we see different covenants being made and established during different periods of time. As believers, I know that we are familiar with the 5 Great Biblical Covenants known as The Noahic Covenant, Abrahamic Covenant, Mosaic Covenant, Davidic Covenant, and the New Covenant—The Covenant of Christ. Each covenant mentioned holds a very powerful yet distinctive statement in history that not only speaks to our past, but speaks to our now, and our prophetic future. The power of covenant begins with creation. The first thing God spoke into the earth was light (Genesis 1:3) the covenant of day and night. God made an agreement with creation that no one can alter. God covenanted with creation and presented himself as THE CREATOR! He spoke it and creation came into agreement with everything God spoke. Until this day creation has not fallen out of agreement with God's covenant.

Martial covenant is one of the most powerful earthly covenants, so much so that the enemy has worked hard to destroy and bring disorder from the beginning between the man and woman covenant. Martial covenant is bilateral; it is a bond and a sealing of two people; both vowing and taking an oath that they will each commit and carry out their covenant agreement collectively and individually. Which is why Satan confronted only Eve in the garden. Satan knew if he would have confronted Adam or the both of them, TOGETHER, he would not have accomplished his mission. But here is the thing, Satan's attack was not against man; he used man to attack God! When God established the martial covenant, between Adam and Eve, he was establishing the first and most important institution on earth, THE FAMILY. Adam and Eve were created to form family relationships (Genesis 1:28). God gave charge of the earth over to man and woman "Be fruitful, and multiply, and replenish the earth, and subdue it: and have DOMINION." Before creation, darkness ruled, God snatched from Satan (darkness and void); created creation and placed the man and woman (family) over earth to rule. Since then, Satan has not stopped trying to kill, steal, and destroy the martial covenant which represents the family unit.

Little did Reggie and I know our covenant relationship begin in 1991 with a long-lasting friendship. After 4 years of dating and shacking, in August of 1998, Reggie proposed to me as we were getting ready to fall asleep one night. Out of the blue he gave me a box and said, "I love you, and will you marry me?" Now, a few months leading up to this we had broken up. I had reached a point in my life where I knew I wanted more out of relationships than shacking up. I had done that for far too long. I placed a demand on the man in Reggie, telling him to man-up or get out! Let the "man" (whomever that was) find me and bride me. It had been four years and if he did not know by now that I was "the one" he wanted to spend the rest of his life with, then I respected that; I was ready to release him to go find "THE ONE." By this time, Reggie had joined the church I took him to on our second date, he had been baptized, delivered from selling drugs, and was faithfully attending church. I believe God was working on his heart as he was mine regarding our life. He did move out and moved back with his mom and I carried on with my life. Releasing him was the best thing I could have done at that time because it forced him to reevaluate what was important to him. Releasing him also gave me a chance to reevaluate my life without him and come to the realization that living without him was not what I wanted, but I had to allow him time to come to the same realization. So, while the proposal was simple and direct, the path to our now was everything but that.

The one piece of knowledge we lacked at the beginning of our marriage was the understanding of covenant. Yes, we went through pre-martial counseling, but covenant was not discussed, explained, or taught at that time. The difference I believe in knowing that marriage was more than just a piece of paper and a name change would have taught us to look to God as the third cord in our marriage and not to other people. The Bible teaches us that a threefold cord is not easily broken (Ecclesiastes 4:12). This only holds true when God the Father, the Son, and the Holy Spirit is the ply-cord holding the marriage together. The moment you step outside of the threefold cord, and invite other people into your marital covenant, the cord is cut and now your hedge of protection is gone! Inevitably giving access to infidelity, lying, sexual perversion and immorality, unforgiveness, anger, frustration, distortion, fear, pride, and other issues. The moment that you cut the cord (notice I said YOU cut the cord) God must stand back until both parties reconnect the cord to Him.

I know the question now becomes can one person's actions cause the cord to be cut? Absolutely! You do not need two pair of scissors to cut a cord. It only takes one. When you step outside of covenant, you have now opened yourself, your spouse, and your marriage up for demonic attack. Once the cord is cut, the demonic realm now has legal rights. Think about it, once Adam and Eve cut the cord in the garden, due to disobedience, it opened them up to the demonic realm. All they knew before then was purity so much so that they did not know they were naked. Eve bit the fruit first and opened her husband up to the attack. I believe if Eve would have rebuked the enemy he would not have had access to Adam or their covenant. Please understand the enemy's attack was against God and what God had established in the earth: martial covenant and the family unit, as a whole. Notice Satan never attacked the covenant God made with creation; he came for the family first. His tricks have not changed, he will always attack one spouse and not both together; if he can get one spouse to give him access to the marriage, he now has a legal ground which is why he did not approach them together. What do you think would have happened if the enemy would have approached the both of them, TOGETHER? Well, the three of them (man, woman, and God). The story would have a different ending. Satan knows that he is powerless against a threefold cord. The only power that he has is the power and access that you give him. Do not give Satan access through dishonesty, infidelity, unforgiveness, double mindedness, perversion, fear of failure, comparison, jealousy, and memory recall. Do not give him access to your covenant. Close every demonic portal!

Covenant is a Lifetime

"The Pharisees also came unto him, tempting him, and saying unto him, Is it lawful for a man to put away his wife for every cause? And he answered and said unto them, Have ye not read, that he which made them at the beginning made them male and female. And saith, For this cause shall a man leave father and mother, and shall cleave to his wife: and they twain shall be one flesh? Wherefore they are no more twain, but one flesh. What therefore God hath joined together, let not man put asunder. They say unto him, Why did Moses then command to give a writing of divorcement, and to put her away? He saith unto them, Moses because of the hardness of your hearts suffered you to put away your wives: but from the beginning, it was not so.
Matthew 19:4-8

Covenant is a lifetime and that is not debatable. Covenant breakers are the only ones that will attempt to debate this! God's plan and standard to end or break covenant is only by death. Jesus gives an exception namely, "fornication" which is martial unfaithfulness which includes adultery or any kind of sexual immorality (Matthew 19:9-12). What we missed in the exception is that it is only permitted because of the hardness of the person's heart (unforgiveness). Let me be clear, I am not insinuating that you should stay in a marriage if one has committed adultery and is a repeat offender (I will go deeper on this issue in the chapter "Forgiving the Unforgivable"). What I am saying is that if you have a hardened heart and a difficult time forgiving, deal with the issues of your heart before you enter a covenant relationship. Trust me, you will need a soft heart to walk this thing out; not a weak heart, but a soft heart (there is a difference). Covenant is a walk into death, until death. You must die to yourself, a continual death, a daily death. Every day I wake up, I command my flesh to die and my spirit man to arise. The power of covenant is coming to the knowledge that it is not just about you, it is actually the death of you and a lifetime partnership with God and your spouse until your earthly death (till death do us part).

Moreover, the moment you give yourself permission to step outside of your covenant, you come into agreement with the "covenant-breaker" spirit and that spirit is rooted in division, accusation, self-gratification, pride, ungodly soul ties, rebellion, and witchcraft. Oh boy, did Reggie and I have to learn this fact the hard way! We struggled within our marriage from 1998 until 2007 because we both had invited the covenant-breaker spirit into our marriage. Nine years of division, accusation, self-gratification, pride, ungodly soul ties, rebellion, and witchcraft. We had no idea what we were doing.

My first encounter with the covenant-breaker spirit was within the first sixty days of our marriage. The enemy knew I had a whore in my heart and had not properly severed ALL ungodly soul ties. Satan did not have to come with any new tricks because I had not dealt with the issues of my heart...I was already an easy target. After months of no communication and me thinking I was good because I had gotten married, out of nowhere I get a visit at my job from my ex-lover, I mean my ex-secret. He was just coming by to check on me and see how I was doing. He said, "you look good. I miss you. Why you changed your number? Well, since you do not want me to have your number, here is mine.

Call me if you need me." All it took was eye to eye contact and he had access to the window of my soul and my thoughts. My soul did not rest until I gave in. All I needed was an excuse to call him, a reason to call, an argument to call, and it did not take long for my soul to get what I wanted. All the enemy ever needs is access to your covenant through one person and now he has legal rights to come in like a flood. Please beware of the covenant-breaking spirit and give no room for it. Operate within your covenant! Anything coming in the form of division, accusation, self-gratification, pride, ungodly soul ties, rebellion, and witchcraft is a sign.

Furthermore, let us discuss witchcraft within the marriage. It is not deep at all, it is plain and simple: the three levels of witchcraft within a marriage are **manipulation, intimidation,** and **control.** If you do not get a clear understanding of these 3 levels, you will unknowingly come into agreement with the covenant-breaking spirit. These are what I like to refer to as "illegitimate authorities." I was operating in all three of them and I did not know it; so, let me help you.

THREE LEVELS OF WITHCRAFT IN A MARRIAGE

*Manipulation
*Intimidation
*Control

- **Manipulation**—the action of manipulating your spouse in a clever way; to manage or influence your spouse skillfully; to suit your purpose or advantage; controlling your spouse or the situation to your own advantage, often unfairly or dishonestly. **This can be done Psychologically and Emotionally.**

- **Intimidation**—to bully or frighten your spouse into submission; inducing fear with threats in order to persuade your spouse to do something you want them to do; to prey on your spouse's weakness. **This can be done Psychologically and Emotionally.**

- **Control**—to dominate every aspect of your marriage; to exercise authorative or dominating influence over your spouse; aggressive rulership or sway over your spouse.
This can be done Psychologically and Emotionally.

When there is an imbalance of power within the marriage, someone is operating in illegitimate authority.

For me, I came into the relationship with an aggressive personality. My grandmother, oldest sister (Trevas) and I moved to the projects when I was 7 years old and Trevas was 9 years old. One day we were living in a big house and the next day we were moving to the projects. I do not think we understood the culture shock we were about to experience at that time. We were new on the block and bus; therefore, my sister and I became easy targets for bullying. One day we did not know our grandmother was standing on the porch watching us, when Trevas and I got off the bus and quickly ran home as we had been doing for few days. My grandmother asked us, "Why y'all running?" I said, "Eugene be bothering us on the bus and he said he gone beat us up when we get off the bus. So, we ran home so we won't get beat up." "Oh yeah," was all she said. The next day, as my sister and I prepared to exit the bus and run home, what a great joy we felt to see my grandmother waiting at the bus stop (so I thought). We got off the bus, and she asked, "Which one is Eugene?" She called him over and asked him, "You want to fight my girls?" I really do not remember his answer, all I remember was my grandmother saying, "SHAWNEY, FIGHT HIM!" "What? Shawney, fight him? But Trevas is the oldest," I said. "I don't care, I said fight him, and you better not lose," she said. Mind you, I was only seven years old, I had never had a fight before, he was a boy, and I was a skinny girl, with long plaits. I went to swinging and crying! When we got home my grandmother called me into her room and I remember her words to me, like it was yesterday. She told me she was proud of me and to never back down from a fight. She said, "Fighting ain't got no rules, you do and use whatever you have to defend you and your sister. You don't let anybody mess with your sister!"

I call that day the "Birth of the Beast." I do not know if I won or loss that fight, all I know is that was the last day me and my sister got chased home from school and everyone knew if you messed with Trevas, you had to see her little-big sister. Although my grandmother meant well, what her request did was birth an aggression in me that only got worse as I got older. I carried this aggressive, defensive behavior with me, into my marriage. Within my marriage, for years, I operated in manipulation, intimidation, and control; unknowingly, coming into agreement with the covenant-breaking spirit, yet again, but on another level…witchcraft. Reggie was no push over, he just did not like confrontation. I knew that and used that to my advantage, in the wrong way.

Remember, covenant is a lifetime! And if you have identified that you have come into agreement (knowingly or unknowingly) with the covenant-breaker spirit, REPENT! First to God, and then to your spouse, and fall out of agreement with the covenant-breaker spirit.

PRAY THIS PRAYER:

Father God, I renounce illegitimate authority and I come into agreement with your spiritual authority of covenant. I renounce the covenant-breaker spirit and come against division, accusation, self-gratification, pride, ungodly soul ties, and witchcraft, in the form of manipulation, intimidation, and control within my marriage, in the Mighty Name of Jesus. I repent for operating in any form of the covenant breaking spirit. I repent for opening myself, my spouse, and my family up to this spirit. I recognize this spirit is not of you, and that it is a demonic attempt to break the martial threefold cord. I decree and declare no weapon formed against my marriage will prosper. I decree all demonic thoughts, ideations, unstable emotions are cast down. I cancel every demonic plan, plot, and scheme. I ask that you seal every demonic portal that I have given legal rights to with the blood of Jesus Christ! And render them of no effect. I ask that you open a heavenly portal over my life and marriage. Release your divine alignment over my marriage. Make every crooked way straight. Release your unconditional love, grace, and mercy. Holy Spirit, I give you permission to deprogram this marriage and to release the spirit of truth over me and my marriage.
In the Mighty Name of Jesus, I pray.
Amen

The Power of Choice

I know the Holy Spirit is going to step on some toes with this section here. I say that because I have heard so many people come into agreement with the covenant-breaker spirit with these words: "I didn't marry the right person; my marriage is/was outside the will of God; I didn't marry my soul-mate; I love my spouse but I'm not in love with my spouse." The power of choice! So, do you think heaven will back your choice, rather good or bad, right or wrong?

God will never take away your ability to choose. The first power of choice was displayed in the Garden of Eden. In the middle of this beautiful garden, a place of peace and seclusion, a place that God created for His divine purpose, God puts an attractive tree that bearded the prettiest fruit without spot or blemish and called it "The Tree of the Knowledge of Good and Evil." God gave simple instruction, regarding that particular tree, when he said, *"you can eat from all the trees in this garden except this one"* (Genesis 2:15-17). Now, God could have placed a locked fence around the tree, he could have placed an angel to stand guard to prevent access to the tree, but that would have taken away their freedom of choice. We all know what happened, they chose to disobey the one commandment God had given and they both ate from the tree. Why didn't God back out on his covenant he had already established with creation and man? Why didn't he just destroy them and start over? Even though their actions displeased God, God did not fall out of love with what he had spoken into existence, he did not fall out of love with what he had created.

Think about it, this had to break God's heart! To create and provide them with everything they needed, to give them access to his true presence, and they chose to disobey his one commandment. They cheated on God, ran and hide themselves! Even though they were wrong in their choice; did heaven walk out on Adam and Eve? No! Instead, God introduces them to "consequence" (Genesis 3:13-19). He did not break his covenant! We do not want to deal with the consequences of our bad choices, so we bail and break covenant and then put God in the middle of it to make us feel justified. I know

And I will give unto thee, the keys to the kingdom of heaven: and whatsoever thou shalt bind on earth shall be bound in heaven: and whatsoever thou shalt loose on earth shall be loosed in heaven.
Matthew 16:19

we usually equate or use this scripture for deliverance but understand that marriage is deliverance. Marriage is the death of self and coming into agreement/covenant with another, so that the two can become one. In Matthew 16:19, Jesus is releasing his delegated authority to us to *"bind" and to "loose"* on earth and demanding heaven to back us. And, he did not put stipulations on it. He did not say only back them if they make the right choice, the right decision, or chose the right person. To be quite honest, there was a long period in my marriage where I thought the same thing: my marriage was not ordained by God, I married the wrong man, I wanted out because I was not happy.

Actually, I had walked away from my marriage and made Reggie sign divorce papers. I packed up all my things and moved to Miami to start a life with another man. I was in bed one night (with this man) and heard someone yelling in my ear to wake up, go back home, it was time, he was ready. The voice was so loud I sat up in the bed asking who was there (like it was a movie scene! Lol). This happened a few times until I finally said who is ready? And the voice said, "Reggie!" Reggie had also attempted to move on with his life, so I had to battle my pride for a few hours, notice I said hours not days, months, years, that is how strong and powerful the voice of the Holy Spirit yelled at me that night. Yes, the Holy Spirit yelled at me, it was not this soft gentle whisper, it was a YELL! On my lunch break, the next day, I called Reggie and when he answered the phone there was a peace that immediately came over me, all I said was, "*I want to come home.*" I will never forget the relief I heard in his voice when he simply said, "come on, *I've been waiting on you.*" I immediately got in my car and came home! Once I got home, we spent the night talking about where we were, and how we had gotten there; we both cried, and God did the rest. We thought we would have to get re-married, but when we checked. we were not divorced. To this day, we do not know what happened to those divorce papers and we did not try to find out.

Heaven will back you even in your wrong decision or wrong choice, but heaven cannot and will not come against God's consequences for YOUR choices. Once your covenant hits heaven, heaven comes into agreement with your covenant and it is bound in heaven until your earthly death. Reggie and I had to deal with some strong and hard consequences, we had to die a thousand deaths, we had to help bare each other's pain, we had to go through "individual deliverance" and then "marriage deliverance," it was not easy, but it was worth it! We are now on the deliverance team at our Church. We are currently taking our first couple through "couples/marriage deliverance." Stop thinking you can break covenant because you married the wrong person and deal with your consequences, go through your processes with your spouse. Never forget "Choices and Consequences" but remember heaven is backing you and His grace is sufficient!

JOURNAL

Your Thoughts & Notes From This Chapter

Chapter Two

HEALING THE WOUNDS WITHIN

If I could re-write the story of my life, I would not. I would keep every page and would not change one experience. However, the one thing I wish I could do differently, I would not have gone into my marriage in broken pieces. My soul was so fragmented (torn & damaged) that I had detached from the main core of who I was and had become…a double-minded, emotional, spiritual, schizophrenic woman. I had so many demonic alters within (anger, unforgiveness, strife, profanity, perversion, lying, manipulation, control, argumentative, violence, rebellion, pride, resentment, rudeness, foolishness, bitterness, rejection, pornography, fornication, and adultery). I did not know who I was; I was having a serious identity crisis. I was truly the "Bag Lady" carrying and holding so much within that my soul was in complete turmoil. I looked good on the outside, but the inside was in disarray. I was so busy making sure I was altogether on the outside that I neglected the most valuable part of me: my inner/spirit man. I needed inner healing!

Inner Healing

"Therefore, we are buried with him by baptism into death: that like as Christ was raised up from the dead by the glory of the Father even so we also should walk in newness of life. For if we have been planted together in the likeness of his death, we shall be also in the likeness of his resurrection: Knowing this, that our old man is crucified with him, that the body of sin might be destroyed, that henceforth we should not serve sin."
Romans 6:4-7

Inner Healing—to be free from the negative emotional effect of painful experience. Mostly caused by people.

The prolonged indwelling of negative emotions or situations that have caused inner wounds evokes continual "emotional warfare" that opens the doors of your mind, will, and emotions to demonic interference. The soul is comprised of three parts: mind, will, and emotions (Psalms 139:4, Proverbs 19:2, Job 7:14-15, Job 6:7, Psalms 35:9, Song of Solomon 1:7, and Jeremiah 13:17). Your soul can become wounded from sin, ungodly soul ties, trauma, divorce, rejection, and abandonment. Inner healing allows your soul to come into alignment with your born-again spirit. Until your soul and born-again spirit comes into alignment with the spirit of the living God (the Spirit of Truth), your demonic alters will continue to control you mind, will, and emotions, causing inner turmoil and a serious identity crisis.

Ideally, we think because we have moved on with life that we have healed from a traumatic or hurtful event. This is far from the truth. Right now, if you look back on that traumatic experience, relationship, or hurtful event and still experience some type of negative emotional response, you have not healed from that wound. You have simply applied a band aid to an open wound and as we know, a band aid is a temporary fix. Think about it: applying a band aid to an open wound will not stop the bleeding nor will it relieve the pain. It may cover the wound a little, but you will still continue to bleed unless you stop the bleeding before applying the band aid. This is exactly how we often time handle inner wounds. We look for a temporary fix or a band aid to cover the wound. That band-aid can be sex, a new relationship, drugs, alcohol, depression, isolation, and over indulgence, which all can become some form of inner turmoil. Your inner turmoil has now become "your bondage" and "your bondage" has now become a stronghold. Negative or toxic emotions are a result of inner turmoil. You cannot and will not function properly or normally if you are breeding a toxic soul (mind, will, and emotions)! I will give you the warning that I wish someone would have given to me: **DO NOT ENTER INTO YOUR MARRIAGE OR ANY NEW RELATIONSHIP UNTIL**

YOU HAVE BEEN SET FREE, FROM A TOXIC SOUL! God created us as emotional beings; therefore, he understands that emotional pain is a part of life. However, improperly dealing with traumatic experiences, relationships, hurtful events, and negative emotions creates a demonic breeding ground giving Satan (and his legion of demons) legal access to your mind, will, and emotions.

Ungodly Soul Ties

There are two areas that quickly give Satan access to our soul to bring forth demonic oppression: ungodly soul ties and a broken heart. Let me put this disclaimer out here: I know we have heard over and over again about soul ties and the different forms of soul ties and how dangerous they are. So much so that most Christians have turned a deaf ear to this subject and refuse to take heed to the warnings (I did too) and it almost cost me my life. So, if you want to keep playing Russian roulette with your soul, skip over this section. I will deal with this oppression head on and with much transparency.

As we know, biblical teachings shows us that there are two forms of soul ties: godly soul ties and ungodly soul ties. A godly soul tie can be described as any relationship, organization, or emotional connection that helps prefect your walk in God or points you to connect to God on a deeper level that increases your spiritual growth. A godly soul tie knits your soul to the Father. While there are a few forms of ungodly soul ties (unhealthy friendships, organizations, fraternities, gangs, unhealthy family relationships), the one I will deal with is the most potent: soul ties formed through fornication and adultery. An ungodly soul tie formed through fornication and adultery is the knitting together of your soul emotionally to another soul through intimate sexual intercourse or communication. An emotional soul tie through communication is just as strong and intimate as sexual intercourse. Spirits of control, witchcraft, manipulation, and domination operate strongly through soul ties formed through fornication and adultery. You may wonder what makes soul ties formed through fornication and adultery so powerful. One word "intimacy" (in-to-me-see). I did a word study on the word "intimacy" and what I found during my word study shocked me and scared me straight! I want to share with you what I found that gave me a clear understanding as to why fornication and adultery forms such a powerful stronghold.

Intimacy (dictionary)—closeness, togetherness; familiarity, affection; confidence, sexual intercourse; personal, private.

Strong's Greek: 2842—Intimacy—Koinonia

Koinonia (Noun-Feminine)—spiritual fellowship, a fellowship in the spirit; communion, partnership; a sharing, intercourse; communication.

Intimacy (Shawney's definition)—spoken and unspoken affections shared inwardly that produces a connection to another's soul and spirit; oneness; the ability to see and connect to the inner man/soul (in-to-me-see); private and personal relation.

Intimacy is powerful! It gives legal access to the most intimate and private part of you (your inner man). Let me explain why Satan has perverted intimacy. He came from intimacy (Heaven) and all his rights to intimacy were revoked when he got expelled from heaven. There is something about intimacy we all long for, well so does Satan and since he cannot have it and we (humans) can, he hates us. Since the beginning, Satan has worked and will not stop working to bring perversion, chaos, confusion, and disruption to intimacy. You also came from intimacy (Heaven). You don't believe me? Let me show you:

Jeremiah 1:5

"Before I formed you in the womb, I knew you; And before you were born, I consecrated you; I have appointed you a prophet to the nation.

Before—during the period of time preceding

Formed—to create something

Womb—birthing chamber

Knew—intimacy

Consecrated—make or declare for divine purpose

This is God speaking directly to Jeremiah. God was not only speaking to Jeremiah about him but also about you and gives us a glimpse into heaven and where we come from. What God is saying is: "I was intimate with you, I knew you before I placed you in the birthing chamber and I consecrated you. I declared you for my divine purpose." We came from spiritual intimacy with the Father and were placed in the birthing chamber through intimacy to bring forth His divine purpose. Satan is the master of perversion (alteration of something from its original intent). If he can pervert intimacy, he can pervert your divine purpose. This perversion started back in the garden. The first human intimate relationship was between God and Adam. There was nothing perverted about this intimacy, it was pure and holy. God CREATED Adam in his image (Genesis 1:27). The ruah breath of God was blown into Adam (spirit to spirit), the intimacy between God and Adam was such a pure, loving, spiritual fellowship that the harmony of man, God, and creation was a powerful force of unity (oneness). This unity was so powerful that Satan immediately begins looking for a way to bring a separation between the intimacy of God and man. It was Satan's way of saying if I cannot have it (intimacy) neither can you, man. God's original intent for intimacy has always been spiritual, not sexual. Which is why Adam and Eve, did not have sexual intercourse until after the fall (Genesis 4:1), they did not need fleshly intimacy from each other because they were connected spiritually, and not fleshly. Spiritual intimacy is more powerful than fleshly intimacy! The fall disconnected their spirit and soul from the purity of intimacy with the Father, producing the start of their soul longing for (fleshly) intimacy.

Women and Soul-ties

The woman has been labeled as being the "most" emotional being in relationships, and for the most part that seemed to be true, until I received a revelation from the Holy Spirit that brought me much clarity and understanding as to why that label appears to be true. Do not get it twisted, men are emotional too they just show and "release" their emotions in a different way. My prayer for my sisters reading this is that you receive a pure understanding of the value, worth, and danger concerning your "pocketbook" (vagina). Yes, there is a danger! The Holy Spirit took me back to the beginning Genesis to show me this and to give me a revelation that forever changed me. Ladies, if you do not get a pure understanding of your value and worth, you will continue to ignorantly operate in the spirit of perversion concerning your "pocketbook" and continue to knit your soul to others through intimacy (verbal and sexual).

Our wombs were blessed to give birth two-fold, spiritual birth and human birth. Technically, Adam was the first to give birth or life to another human. Adam was created with the female in him. Genesis 1:27 says *"In the image of God created him; male and female created he them."* **Genesis 2:21 says** *"And the Lord God caused a deep sleep to fall upon Adam, and he slept: and he took one of his ribs and closed up the flesh instead thereof; And the rib, which the Lord God had taken from man, made he a*

woman, and brought her unto the man." Sounds like a birth by way of C-section, well rib-section performed by the Lord God (the first surgeon) on Adam, birthing forth Eve. Now, I do not know what happened during Adam's recovery process because the Bible does not give details, but my sanctified imagination tells me that his healing process was very painful and Adam did not take it too well. I say that because in Genesis 3:16, the Lord places this sorrow on Eve because of the part she played in the fall of man. (***"Unto the woman he said, I will greatly multiply thy sorrow and they conception; in sorrow thou shalt bring forth children;"***) Yes, Eve is the first MOTHER of all humanity, but Adam was the first human, he was the first and he bought forth the first (Eve) and in return Eve brought forth Adam's first seed Cain, which is the first human birth by the woman. The seed of the man is released into the womb of the woman through sexual intercourse....pause: for my analytical thinkers, I know science has now came forth with different forms of conception that does not require physical contact between the man and the woman like artificial insemination, IVF, and surrogacy, but there still had to be a form of intercourse in order for the seed to come forth from the man for all those procedures.

NEWS FLASH: any form of ejaculation from the man is sexual intercourse even if it is with his hand; masturbation is a form of sexual intercourse. So, the seed of the man is released into the womb of the woman; our wombs are the "carrier." What do we carry? We carry not only our emotions, hurts, pains, joys, sorrows, we carry everything the male releases into our womb when he ejaculates INTO us. He is not just releasing his sperm into you, he is releasing his strength, his anger, his frustrations, his disappointments, his fantasies, his lust, his perversion, his whatever he is feeling at that time INTO you. Which is why most times, once a man releases, he is exhausted or feels like weights have been lifted off him; he rolls over and can go right to sleep and we are wide awake ready to talk (LOL). It does not matter if he has on a condom or not, he is still releasing INTO you. Sometimes for the man the release is so strong and powerful, the enemy tricks us into believing our "pocketbook" is the bomb. When the truth is you just had a bomb released into you and you do not even know it. I remember having a sexual encounter with this dude, with the false illusion that my "pocketbook" was the bomb because of the release he had just experienced during intercourse, not realizing he had just released a bomb into me. That night, I had a dream that was so violent it involved me murdering someone and all of a sudden, my aggression grew strong, I began to have murderous thoughts. In my anger, I would threaten people with words like "I'll kill you," "I hate you," "I'll split your head to the white meat." I started carrying a blade, a knife around with me waiting and longing for the chance to use it. A few years after our encounter that dude was arrested for shooting someone. What he released into my soul that night was a murderous spirit. The murderous spirit's cousins are bitterness, hatred, unforgiveness, anger, malice, spite, jealousy, revenge, and retaliation…I had found myself operating in all of the above.

We have been bewitched to believe the lie that our "pocketbook" holds the power and that is the way to get a man and keep a man. Jay-Z and R. Kelly have a song called "The Power of the P.U.S.S.Y." (not my language LOL) and when this song came on in the club (mostly the strip club) the women would come alive and go into a trance trying to get an arouse out of the men. The song should have been called "The Power of the E.J.A.C.U.L.A.T.I.O.N." The power is in what is being released INTO you. The bigger the womb bag lady, the bigger the release! Have you ever wondered why you can give your man all the sex he wants, good sex at that and he still masturbates? I will tell you why, because he is addicted to the release, he is addicted to the ejaculation. Instead of dealing with his emotions, he looks to release those emotions either in you or his hand. This is dangerous because you do not know what is being released into your soul or what you are knitting your soul with. There is a powerful give and take exchange during this process; he gives through the release and when he pulls out, he pulls out with a piece of your soul and takes it with him. It is never just sex; it is a soul-tie!

Men and Soul-ties

Most men think soul-ties cannot necessarily attach to them because they are the ones releasing into the women, so they good. This is what God gave me, and when he gave it to me, I wanted to back out of this topic because I thought it was a little too transparent for the religious spirit that operates in so many believers. Yet, the Holy Spirit said to write it like he gave it to ME and do not try to dress it up in a nice suit. Therefore, I will be raw, real, and very transparent with explaining men and soul-ties. My prayer for my brothers reading this section is that the spirit of lust and perversion will be demolished through the word of wisdom and knowledge to bring forth a pure understanding of the part that they play in the soul of the woman AND the man. Remember the woman came from you, man.

I want to show you the "power of penetration" and the "power of ejaculation"…how Satan grips the soul of the man through penetration and ejaculation. How you can become addicted to these two, causing the spirit of the whore or you may want to call it the spirit of the dog to become lodged into your soul.

> **Penetration (dictionary)**—the action or process of making a way through or INTO something or someone; a define depth in which something has gotten through; the ability to discern deeply and acutely; deep insight.

The mind of the man will always remember its first penetration. Doctors have determined that there is a chemical released in the brain during penetration called *dopamine*, it is referred to as the "feel-good" chemical and the chemical that binds two people together. Sounds familiar? I refer to it as the "soul-tie" chemical. There is a show I watch called "Intervention." It is about people who are addicted to drugs wherein their families are coming to together in the form of an intervention to get their loved one help and enter them into drug rehab. During the show, they do these interviews with the person addicted to drugs and the most common thing I hear them say is they spend years addicted to drugs because they are chasing that first "high" feeling. Well, most men spend years chasing that first "penetration" feeling, that feel-good feeling with any woman that would let them penetrate. Not knowing that you are binding your soul with every woman you are penetrating. The Holy Spirit revealed to me that the dopamine chemical works as a silent killer of the mind. It releases an invasion or perversion into your mind, will, and emotions. It wreaks havoc in your soul! After that first penetration, you find yourself engulfed in this fantasy world of "I gotta have it; I cannot live without it" and I will take it from whoever gives it to me!"

Brother, every time you penetrate you are piercing into deep insight, deep intimacy (in-to-me-see) which creates a deep-rooted bond to that soul. You are not just penetrating the vagina; you are penetrating the soul! You my brother have just entered into an unholy union. An unholy union is an illegal joining or uniting of two souls through sexual intercourse. Yes, you have illegally married that soul! Just take a moment and think of all the souls you have penetrated and wreak havoc on………that is how many souls you have illegally married. You probably will never know the damage you have caused to the soul of those women! Every time you engage in sex outside of marriage, you are forming a bond and while it may not mean anything to you at the time but sex, it is never just sex! It is a soul tie! **1st Corinthians 6:16 says:** *"What? Know ye not that he which is joined to a harlot is one body? For two, saith he, shall be one flesh."* Through fornication and adultery, you are waging war against your soul. **1st Peter 2:11 verifies this and it says:** *"Dearly beloved, I beseech you as strangers and pilgrims, abstain from fleshly lust, which war against the soul."* Brother, not only are you waging war against your soul but also the soul of the woman, through penetration and ejaculation (a double whammy for the woman). Because the male gets two releases, 1st through penetration and 2nd, through ejaculation. The power of penetration is the first stage of the soul tie when the chemical of dopamine is released.

Now, once you penetrate the soul, you do not know what lies waiting for you in that soul. You do not know what was deposited into that soul prior to your entry. As I explained above, one of the gateways to the soul of the woman is through the vagina. In my opinion, this gateway holds the most dangerous and powerful bond of soul ties. So, let us breakdown the power of ejaculation.

> **Ejaculation (dictionary)**—the act or process of a sudden and explosive release from the male reproductive tract; the final stage of the male stimulation.

Sexual sin produces a strong sexual appetite. There are more than two sexual sins (fornication and adultery) that feed the sexual appetite including pornography, masturbation, homosexuality, lesbianism, phone sex, sex-texting (sexting), and incest. As explained in the definition above, the final stage of the male stimulation is a release. There is a transferring of spirit that can take place during this release. Psychologically, men have been taught at an early age not to show their emotions as it is a sign of weakness. Sadly, this teaching has jacked most men up! So instead of displaying their true emotions, they become walking stuffed animals. I call it the "Stuffed Animal Syndrome." A stuffed animal is nice looking and handsome on the outside, but they (men) could be stuffed with anger, disappointment, rejection, abandonment (fatherless), hurt, pain, and the biggest one of all, FEAR! Fear of being labeled a sissie, weak, not masculine if he shows emotions, by crying. This usually starts at a very early age. While crying is the most sacred release, for the young boy it is frowned upon and starts a disconnect of the mind and heart. The mind knows it is wrong to say and do certain things that you know will hurt the woman, but the mind sends a signal to the heart not to show the emotion; suck it up like a man because this is what you were taught as a boy.

Eventually, the boy will not allow the man to release the most sacred release, tears. Man, this is the start of "perversion" and the emotionless man, that I call the stuffed animal syndrome. This is the first exposure of the young boy to perversion. Satan repeats this cycle with every boy because we have been falsely taught perversion is only related to the sexual appetite. Perversion is the alteration of something from its original course, meaning or state to a distortion or corruption of what was first intended. The mind of the boy has been altered to think showing emotions is a sign of weakness. Meanwhile, the little girl can cry; she can release her emotions. Subsequently, little girls are often labeled "emotional creatures" or "too emotional." We were all created by the same God and he created us all as emotional beings. It is the releasing of our emotions that has become perverted, in some ways.

And, how does this relate to soul ties? Glad you asked. The mind, body, and spirit know and functions in the order of its original design and knows that a release must take place. Thus, the mind and body of the boy begins to search for a release at an early age and since he has already been introduced to emotional perversion, the door way for sexual perversion is easily found in the mind and body of the boy, most times through masturbation. Once the mind and body of the boy experience its first explosive release, through masturbation, sexual perversion has now captivated the mind of the boy and the pureness of the boy's mind is infiltrated with self-gratification. For most boys, this becomes their form of release, they hold in all of their emotions until they find that private time to release. This behavior is usually carried from the boy to the man, from the man into the soul of the woman.

The transferring of spirits can take place during this stage depending strongly on what has taken place between the two souls prior to their sexual encounter. Depending on what the soul of the women is carrying and what emotions the man has stuffed on the inside of him and releases into the soul of the woman. Another transfer can happen when the male pulls out, he pulls out a piece of the woman's soul with him! Brothers, have you ever wondered why you can meet a woman and be cool with her, kick it with her, Netflix and chill with her, establish a friendship; then, the relationship moves to having sex; and, after sex you still feel the same way about the woman (she is just a friend). But the woman is now obsessed with you, possessive, gets all emotional with you (falling in love) and you think, "I thought we were just kicking it?" Well, this is part of the reason…you have taken a piece of her soul and probably the souls of many others before you from her and while you feel like it is nothing you are carrying a piece of her with you; and, now she feels entitled to you. There has been a spiritual exchange and because you have been taught not to feel you do not realize it. An exchange is defined as the act of giving one thing and receiving another in return. Do not think for one minute that you can make a deposit into the soul of the woman and not get something back in return. It just may take you longer to feel it, realize it, or know it. You may be carrying many soul-ties and need a serious soul detox! It is never just sex! It is a soul-tie!

Soul Detoxification

The most common question I am asked when counseling a married person or a person who is currently dating is "Can I still have a soul tie, if I have moved on and am now married?" My response: just because you have moved on from a painful situation, traumatic event, relationship, or sexual encounter that does not mean you have properly dealt with the effects from it. Yes, you have moved on, but I guarantee the effects are still showing up in your present through patterns, behaviors, and vicious cycles.

When I gave my life to Christ (for real) in 2007, I had been married to Reggie for nine years and sometime around 2009, I began to seek God on a much deeper level and my prayer became God show me and help me to deal with the hidden things in my heart. At that time, I had been saved (for real) for about two years. I keep saying I became saved for real because up until then, I thought I was saved, doing all those nasty and hidden things I really thought "once saved, always saved," "once baptized, always saved." Not knowing I had joined in with Satan in perverting Salvation and God's grace! I kept having these ungodly thoughts and dreams of me having sex with different people, some known and some unknown. During this process, the Holy Spirit revealed to me that my soul was fragmented and I needed to go through a soul detox deliverance to bring back the pieces of my soul that had been given to other people. Before we go into the soul detox process, let me acknowledge that every person's process is different and at different depths. I will only provide a guideline, but you will need to seek God on how you should proceed with your process.

Prayerfully, this guideline will give you a start...

Soul Detoxification—the process of removing toxic people and events physically, emotionally, mentally, and spiritually from your soul; releasing all past hurts and the effects; releasing impurities.

Signs you may need Soul Detox

1. **Emotional trigger:** emotional triggers are anytime a song, movie, event, or thought of an experience causes a negative emotional response this is a sign of an open wound. This includes crying, withdrawal or isolation, lashing out in anger, feeling of rejection, or a complete emotional shut down.

2. **Over reaction or magnification:** over exaggeration of a situation. This includes being argumentative, always giving rebuttals, defensive and playing the victim, gossip, and/or slander.

3. **Unforgiveness:** holding a grudge against someone for something that happened in the past, present, or future. This includes having a hard time letting things go. Always bringing past situations up in new situations. Always injecting pain from your past to justify inappropriate behavior.

4. **Memory recall:** a constant replay of different negative memories. This includes comparing

current situations to past events. Only recalling bad memories to use as manipulation.

5. **Insecurity:** negative emotions that take a toll on your confidence. This includes giving power to negative words spoken to you or about you. Believing what everyone thinks of you and false identity. Self-sabotage.

6. **Relationship to Relationship:** you have a hard time staying or navigating relationships. This includes family relationships. It is always the other person's fault why the relationship did not work. Easy to get into a new relationship, but hard to stay in it. Jumping from relationship to relationship easily. Using new relationship as healing for old wounds. Multiple divorces.

7. **Vicious Cycles:** habitual bad habits that destroy relationships and your quality of life. This includes a repeated cycle that ends relationships negatively. You also play the victim in these situations. Slandering people that you have ended relationship with. Lying to make the other person(s) look bad. Fault finding in every relationship or situation. Habitually critical of others. A spin cycle from chaos to chaos. Drama follows you. Self-Sabotage.

As I stated earlier, each person's process is different. The beginning of every process is acknowledgement. My spiritual father, Apostle Mark T. Jones, said something so powerful…"You can't fix something you're not willing to face or acknowledge. You must face it to fix it!" The enemy will hold you in bondage to the same situation with one thing, DENIAL. I encourage you to be honest with yourself! My soul detox did not happen overnight or in one deliverance session. I started it by asking the Holy Spirit to bring back to my remembrance every painful, traumatic event, relationship, and sexual encounter I had experienced. To reveal the wounds my Band-Aids were hiding. I wrote down each experience, each person (including family) that had impacted and caused damaged to my soul. Things that I had completely forgotten, buried, and covered with a band-aid came to the surface. At first, I tried to stop the emotions attached to each event from coming up and the Holy Spirit quickly corrected me and told me as they come up to let go of the negative emotions attached to it (anger, hurt, pain, self-sabotage, guilt, shame, embarrassment, brokenness, broken heartedness, lies I told to cover it up, disappointment, discouragement, and inadequacies). I had to carry my journal around because the memories would come at any time. I would be riding in my car, praying and the Holy Spirit would bring something to the surface. This went on for about 3-4 months. I had about thirty pages when I finished.

Afterwards, I fasted and prayed asking God to heal and deliver my will, emotion, and mind from each negative event. I repented. I forgave people who never asked for forgiveness, but who had hurt me (knowing and unknowingly). The Holy Spirit told me to end my fast by burning the pages of my heart and to never bring them up again unless I am using them as a testimony to help someone else. I took the pages, put them on my grill outside, and burned them. I could not understand why he told me to burn the pages and honestly, I felt a little stupid. Once the pages finished burning, they began to turn into ashes and I heard the Holy Spirit say, "I am giving you beauty for your ashes," and at that moment, I lost it, the tears would not stop flowing, my tongue would not stop giving him worship and a new heavenly language was birthed in me. These new tears were tears of joy! The breaking and healing I experienced in that moment was life changing.

Ways to Detox your Soul

1. Acknowledgement

2. Fasting and praying

3. Avoid negative thoughts, words, and conversation.

4. Uncover your hidden secrets and lies
5. Uproot all roots of bitterness and toxicity in your life
6. Repentance
7. Forgive those who hurt you. The ones that asked for forgiveness and you are still holding a grudge and the ones who have never asked for forgiveness. Love them like it never happened.
8. Divine alignment with the Word of God
9. Only use those negative experiences as testimonies
10. When the negative emotions try to rise up, remind yourself that you have forgiven them, and you are healed, delivered, and set free from those emotions. And put praise on it!

Heavenly Father,

I thank you for revelation of your Word. I decree and declare that my soul belongs to you and I repent for giving pieces of my soul away through emotional pain, sexual immorality, my free will, and un-ordained relationships. I call back the fragmented pieces of my soul to divine alignment with your Word. Father, I release myself from every unholy alliance that I have formed through fornication, adultery, pornography, masturbation, incest, fantasies, sorrow of heart, broken heart, unforgiveness, bitterness, toxic emotions, no emotions, self-sabotage, lying, manipulation, and domination. I release my soul from every bad experience of hurt, pain, rejection, abandonment, and trauma. Father, release your Holy Fire to consume every fiery dart of the enemy that has lodged into the depths of my soul and causes me to have toxic emotions or no emotions. The blood of Jesus is applied to the door post of my mind and covers the windows of my soul, allow complete healing and deliverance to take place within me. I come against the demon of memory recall with the blood of Jesus and forbid it to operate in the corners of my mind. I decree and declare that I have the mind of Christ and I shall think on things that are lovely, honest, just, pure, and of good report. I repent for my perverted sexual appetite, perverted sexual character, and sexual desires. I call my loins to be girded up with truth and my body to wear the whole armor of God! The blood of Jesus is against the Incubus and Succubus spirit and I command they come under the arrest of the Holy Spirit and shall no longer infiltrate my dreams and violate me. I revoke the legal access that I had given to Satan through rebellion and disobedience. I release every person I have come into unholy matrimony with through sexual contact physically, vocally, psychologically, and emotionally. Allow the Sword of the Spirit to cut every demonic cord and server the bands of wickedness. I call my will, mind, and emotions back into alignment with you, Heavenly Father. I belong to you and I thank you for loving me.

In Jesus Name,

Amen.

JOURNAL

Your Thoughts & Notes From This Chapter

Chapter Three

ROOT UP, TEAR DOWN, AND DESTROY TO REBUILD

See, I have this day set thee over the nations and over the kingdoms, to root out, and to pull down, and to destroy, and to throw down, to build, and to plant.
Jeremiah 1:10

The life that you have is the life that you have built. If you do not like the life that you have, root up, tear down, destroy, and rebuild. After ten years of marriage and being in the wilderness, this was the word of the Lord spoken to Reggie and I concerning our lives and our marriage. By now, we had been together for fourteen years and the thought of tearing it all down to start over was overwhelming, but when we turned and looked back at what we had built, we realized we had built a relationship without a firm foundation and without walls. Coming to terms with this realization hit us like a ton of bricks. We both were damaged and in return had damaged each other in the process of trying to love each other from a contaminated place. The one thing we had left in us was the good in both of us; and, we realized that the good outweighed the bad, so we decided to root it all up, tear it all down, destroy the entire foundation, and REBUILD.

My prayer is that throughout this chapter the root of dysfunction, disorder, and dishonor will be uprooted, and the Holy Spirit will lay the groundwork to build a firm foundation for your marriage. I pray fear will not keep you in bondage and that you will not be afraid to tear it all down and start over! I release a start over and a reset anointing over every marriage that needs it!

Root Up

> **Root Up** ↑ is to uproot all deep-rooted issues that have caused bitterness, anger, and deception to manifest within the marriage; to identify the operating system of dysfunction and remove it completely.

You will need to be very strategic and direct with this process because it is part of the foundation. In the natural, before construction can take place they have to first go in and remove the trees and its roots. They remove the debris and everything that can hinder the building process. Tree roots go very deep into the ground and if not properly uprooted will likely take root and grow again and can cause some serious damage to the structure, if built upon. The root of dysfunction also goes very deep and was probably imbedded in your soul as a child. The one thing that holds true for dysfunction is dysfunction begets dysfunction. You will get nowhere trying to build on top of the root of dysfunction. Our process of uprooting started with identifying the dysfunction we were exposed to as children through our upbringing.

The first dysfunction being we were both raised in single-parent homes…him, all his childhood and me, over half of my childhood. This upbringing produced a strong spirit of independency within the both of us. Even though we were married, we both thought we did not need each other and could do it on our own. There was no sense of oneness within our marriage. He had his own agenda and I had mine. Forget being on the same page, we were both in different books; my book and his book; never OUR book. Therefore, we had to uproot our pattern of independency and get in the same book, the book of dependency (the Bible), so we could find the same page. God showed us, if our dependency was not on Him, we would never be able to depend on each other and submit to the proper order of marriage.

Another area of dysfunction was poverty. We both came into our marriage with a poverty mind set. Not just financially, but also mentally and spiritually. Yes, we had a roof over our head, we both had jobs, our kids had food to eat, we both drove nice cars, but we lacked discipline. The lack of discipline and being a good steward produces a self-sabotage spirit and gives access to the spirit of lack—financially, mentally, and spiritually over your life. The spirit of poverty is deep rooted in a lack of value, lack of growth, poor decision making, unworthiness, selfishness, borrowing, always looking for the easy way out or the come up, poor in spirit, habitual government assistance, lack of tithing, poor financial decisions, becoming a shopaholic, and hoarding. We had to first acknowledge this spirit was active within our marriage and lay an axe to the root of it. This spirit was broken off our marriage through giving; we were challenged to give ten percent of our tithes, ten percent in offering, and ten percent in love offerings. So, instead of just giving ten percent, we gave thirty percent of our income each pay period for three months. As I stated before, everybody's process is different; thus, once you identify the root, seek the Holy Spirit on how to uproot it.

There was also a strong dysfunction in our communication. Our love language was so contaminated it affected our natural communication. Our communication was filled with disagreements, arguments, fault finding, disrespect, dishonor, and finger pointing. We could not agree on anything; and we both went to outside sources to expose each other faults and to deal with what we could not deal with within ourselves. Satan is the master of magnification and his greatest weapon of magnification is corrupt communication! If he can corrupt the communication between the husband and wife, it divides the entire family. Division within the family is a major dysfunction. Because we both were exposed to division within our own families, we carried division into our marriage and let me just tell you, saying I DO, does not uproot corrupt communication and division. You must develop a pattern of good communication, good listening skills, and good responses to uproot the dysfunction of corrupt communication. We had to both give up our right to be right and listen to each other's heart.

Pray for a **SHUT-UP** Anointing!

Honestly, I had to pray hard for a shut-up anointing! When you are trained as a child to defend your territory at all cost and there are no rules to defending your territory, the hardest thing for me to do was to give up the fight and let him win. I had to realize we were on the same team, and when he wins, I win! I had a problem with listening because I was so busy trying to be heard, I could not hear him or God. It took months of counseling for Reggie and I to learn effective communication skills. It was a deep-rooted system that we had to uproot before we began to lay the new foundation of our marriage.

These are just a few of the challenges we faced in identifying the root cause of our dysfunction. I encourage you to not be afraid to address the hard things like family curses, generational dysfunctions, and division that have now become your norm. Do not be afraid to pray for the shut-up anointing and ask for new ears to hear your spouse. If you cannot hear your spouse, there is no way you will be able to hear God. Do not let Satan trick you into thinking you are hearing from God when you cannot even hear your spouse. If God is speaking to you, then believe he is speaking to you about YOU and not about your spouse! Identify your system of dysfunction and uproot it.

Tear Down

Tear Down ↓ **is** to pull apart by force; to rip apart the built-up deception; to pull down, pluck up, demolish suddenly; to destroy and/or breakdown fortified places.

Before I go into what the Holy Spirit gave me regarding the tearing down process within the marriage, I want to make clear that I am in no way eluding that men are blameless and not responsible in the tear down process. I simply want to show you biblically how we (my sisters) were given the keys and authority, especially in this area. God has graced Reggie and I to do couples deliverance and during one of our sessions with this couple that had only been marriage for about five years but were facing some trying times within their marriage and on the verge of divorce, Reggie begin to minister to the male. He shared with him how I played a big role in his deliverance and how I had helped build him into the man he is today. He admitted he was not perfect, but he was better because of me. Honestly, at first, his statement made me feel real uncomfortable because my first thought was not I…..but GOD! I was about to stop my husband and bring what I thought was correction and the Holy Spirit told me to SHUT UP! I am telling you the shut-up anointing is real! I did just that (SHUT-UP) and allowed Reggie to continue to minister to this husband regarding the part I played and was not aware of in his deliverance process, not just for him, but also for our marriage. I watched a breaking take place in that husband as his pride was exposed and the walls begin to come down.

Proverbs 14:1 says, *"The wise woman builds her house, but the foolish tears it down with her own hands."* Ladies, we hold the keys to make the home a place of refuge, peace, and joy. We also hold the keys to tear it down! There is no doubt we have a level of wisdom upon our lives, that some may refer to as a "woman's intuition." If you can tap into the godly side of your intuition, it can give you access to godly wisdom and produce a strong tear-down anointing. Understanding, the Bible speaks of three different kinds of wisdom in James 3:13-17…*earthly (worldly) wisdom, sensual wisdom, and godly wisdom*. For years, I operated in earthly and sensual wisdom, which brought envy, strife, confusion, and much evil into my home. It was not until I tapped into godly wisdom, that a pure, peaceable, easy to intreat, full of mercy and good fruit, without partially, and without hypocrisy wisdom and love was released over my marriage and home. So, let us dive in!

Ladies, make no mistake about it, SATAN HATES US!! He knows that we possess weapons on the inside of us that abolish and annihilate darkness. If the enemy can keep us spiritually ignorant to the power we have to tear down, he is winning the battle. If he can keep us in conflict and unaware of our true identity as a wise woman, we will unknowingly work with Satan to destroy and tear down not just our home but the male (the head) as well. Satan usually starts at an early age of the women to put conflict in the heart of the women towards the man. Many women are molested, raped, prostituted, abused, left to raise their children alone, misused, and broken hearted, by a man. This attack is strategically aimed at the identity and heart of the woman. You may ask why? Never forget Genesis 3:15, when God put "enmity" (hostile or deep- seated hatred) between Satan and the women. The rivalry between Satan and the women will continue until the day of Christ's return.

Yet and still, we hold some powerful tools against the enemy. The tool I want to arm you with is the "power to tear down." Tear down strongholds and destroy the fortified places within your marriage. Strongholds are incorrect thinking patterns that do not line up with the spirit of truth. This area was strong within my marriage. The enemy was holding us in bondage to the guilt, shame, and embarrassment of our past failures and past sins. I had to gird up my home in prayer and warfare. At first, I was ashamed to let Reggie hear me praying and interceding for him and our marriage. I would always wait until he was not home and if he was home, I would pray quietly. The Holy Spirit dealt with me one day as I was praying softly and said let him hear you. Out of nowhere, a war cry raised up out of my belly and I begin to pray, bind, loose, and release over Reggie and our marriage. When I finished and opened my eyes, I saw my husband sitting on the bed behind me in tears. I knew at that moment something had broken in him and our marriage.

Once I tapped into godly wisdom, God begin to strategically show me how to tear down those fortified places within our marriage through prayer and intercession. It was as if things begin to fix themselves. I did not have to argue, cuss, nor fuss over everything Reggie was doing wrong or not willing to address within himself. I would simply take it to God in prayer. I am laughing at myself right now because that sounds so cliché, but it is the truth. The guilt, shame, and embarrassment were so strong the enemy would use anybody and any reason he could to grip us and hold us in the bondage to our past.

During part of our healing and deliverance process, we shared some of our past sins with our spiritual leaders at that time. Confessing our faults played a huge part in our process because it helped uproot the spirit of secretism off our marriage and family bloodline. I am not sharing this to bring shame to a leader or to bring correction to that leader only to show how the enemy tried to hold us in bondage to our past sins and mistakes. Well, this leader started using scenarios and situations we had shared with him in his messages. No, our names were not used, but our scenarios were being shared in what we thought were a negative way. As a result, we exited that ministry; and our past was still being told to others. At one point, our past was used against my own sister to bring negative exposure to me and my husband. Unknowingly, this leader had joined in with Satan in his attempts to keep us in bondage to our past sins and mistakes. It took much prayer, fasting, and uprooting from that ministry to bring deliverance to the incorrect thinking pattern regarding our past sins and mistakes. That process started and ended with me.

    We started our journey to healing and deliverance, I believe, by God sending us to that ministry to break off the guilt, shame, and embarrassment from our testimony. We had to hear how disgusting our past sins were by having them preached across the pulpit…for God to show us how he would use all of that for His glory! It helped birth a spirit of transparency in me! I begin to say, "Oh no, devil, you will not use our story in a negative way! We will tell our own story! I asked God to give me the wisdom I needed to tear down those triplets (guilt, shame, and embarrassment) off our marriage.

Moreover, instead of assisting the enemy in tearing down my husband and our marriage concerning our past sins and mistakes, I began to speak life into him and our marriage. I began to tell him how great he was and how much he had overcome as a man. I began to remind him of how many marriages could never survive what we had survived. I began to talk to him about those secret things he had a hard time discussing with me and hearing come across the pulpit. When he felt angry or defeated regarding our past being used in a message, I begin to preach that same message back to him and showed him how the blood of Jesus had covered us and kept us. The Holy Spirit began to give me wisdom in how to handle those triplets and how to not let the negative words take root. I started telling all our hidden secrets and sharing my testimony with the praise team and whomever I could. This ministered healing and deliverance to me, my husband, and our marriage. What the enemy meant for bad, God would use for His glory! That began to tear down and demolish the walls of guilt, shame, and embarrassment. It took the Holy Spirit telling me to SHUT-UP to bring forth this revelation.

My beloved sisters, we have a calling and anointing on our lives to tear down…we can choose to use that calling and anointing either foolishly or wisely. I had foolishness in me for a long time and I tore down my marriage and my husband with control, anger, unforgiveness, adultery, by being argumentative, fault finding, and having corrupt communication. My deliverance brought about deliverance for my house on another level. My deliverance birthed forth a new oil in my home, a new fragrance. A fragrance of peace, a fragrance of gentleness, a fragrance of pure love. The Oil of Joy was released over my home! I encourage you to become that wise woman and build your home. Tear down every stronghold through prayer and intercession. Become your husband's intercessor, let him hear you praying for him, tearing down strongholds, and cover your home with the fire of prayer.

Destroy to Rebuild

Know that it is never too late to recover what seems to be lost through rebuilding. You can regain trust once it is destroyed. You can love through disappointments. You can put the pieces of your life and marriage back together again. You can forgive the unforgiveable. You can push past the pain to promise. I would like to make this section comparable to having a house gutted out and rehabbed. We have this couple at our church that have a construction company that often shows the before and after pictures of their work. The outside and the inside of the house before pictures are always a mess and often look unfixable. The frame of the house is still put together, but it is broken and bruised from years of abuse and/or abandonment. The interior is pretty much the same, run down, and in need of some tender-loving care. In the before pictures, it is hard to see any beauty, I mean you must have a creative mind and creative eyes to see the good in something so ugly to the natural eye.

And most times, when you see the house after it is completed, it is almost unrecognizable from the before pictures. The after-effects are that of a beautiful masterpiece. All you see is the beauty of the aftermath. That is exactly what the destroy-to-rebuild process will look like. The frame of the marriage is still put together, but it is broken, bruised, mistreated, and misused from years of dishonor, fighting, unforgiveness, bad decision making, poverty mind-set, corrupt communication, division, and ungodly soul ties; it has basically became the devil's playground. You must go in and gut all that out! Do not start with your spouse start with you! Deal with what is on the inside of you. Before you can rebuild your marriage, you must destroy and uproot everything within you that brings contention or has brought contention into the marriage. Deliverance for your marriage starts with you, not your spouse. If you cannot identify your areas of deliverance but can easily see and point out your spouse's faults, then you need to start with uprooting your pride and take it from there.

I must admit starting with me was hard. I did not know where to start. I had been in bondage to myself for so long uprooting me was something I did not want to do or knew how to do. I had been me for so long I could not wrap my mind around becoming a new me. I begin to pray that God show me myself. It sounds like a simple prayer, right? That was the most powerful prayer I ever prayed! God begin to open my eyes to me and deal with me. I was so disgusted with myself, I called the people closest to me one by one, crying, asking them why they did not tell me I was so jacked up on the inside. Everybody's response was the same: "Shawney, we could not tell you anything without you being ready to fight for hearing the truth." That indeed was a sad reality I had to face and deal with before I could move forward in rebuilding me and my marriage. I had to destroy every fortified place I had built around myself to hide the true issues, hurt, pain, and dysfunction within me. It was time for me to stop playing church, stop playing with myself, and most of all, stop playing with God and let him heal and deliver me. It was the most vulnerable experience I have ever been through. What I thought was my strength was exposed as my weakness.

As we were going through our individual deliverance little did we know this process started rebuilding the foundation of our marriage. We did not care what it looked like from the outside. We knew from the outside we looked jack up, as if we were headed to divorce court, but we also knew that we had to work from the inside out. We did not touch the outside for a long time. We did not try to change what people saw from the outside or what they knew or thought they knew. We did not try to defend what people were saying because they were right! Once we came through our individual deliverance together, we came out with a new foundation, new interior, new mind-set, new eyes, new ears, and a new heart and we began to build off of that. We did not have to clean the exterior, the Holy Spirit did that. So, what am I saying about the rebuilding process? It is an inside job!

PRAYER

Heavenly Father, I thank you for anointing me to root out, tear down, and destroy to rebuild! Through the Word of knowledge, I thank you for laying the axe to the root of evil, bitterness, anger, deception, and dysfunction that has functioned in my marriage and family blood line. Let your Holy fire burn up every evil and wicked root in the Name of Jesus. Let all spirits rooted in rejection, pride, independency, poverty, and corrupt communication be uprooted, cut, and severed in the Mighty Name of Jesus. Tear down and demolish every fortified place. Break up the grounds of my heart, all my past hurts, guilt, shame, embarrassment and release the Balm of Gilead over my marriage. I decree and declare divine alignment to the will of God for my life and my marriage. Jehovah Gibbor, release the warring angel Michael and his army to assist me in battle as I rebuild. I will work as Nehemiah did building with one hand and fighting with the other hand. Teach my hands to war and my fingers to fight. The Peace of God shall be my portion during this process. I am equipped with the sword of the spirit and I come into agreement with Heaven concerning my marriage and my destiny. I renounce fear and anxiety and call forth a cease and desist to chaos and confusion in my marriage and my home. I renounce ignorance and ask that you release your wisdom, revelation, and understanding. I thank you for hearing me and assisting me.

In Jesus Name,

Amen.

JOURNAL

Your Thoughts & Notes From This Chapter

Chapter Four

THE FALSE PERCEPTION OF MARRIAGE

Perception—the ability to see, hear, or become aware of something through the senses; a mental impression; a belief or opinion based on how things seem.

Perception is everything! It plays a very important role in life and relationships. Perception dictates your responses, thoughts, feelings, and actions toward your spouse. The one thing that can shift your perception in your marriage is conflict, especially unresolved conflict. Because I was raised in a single parent home, TV helped shape my perception of marriage. James and Florida Evans from "Good Times" and Cliff and Clair Huxtable from "The Cosby Show" were my examples of what marriage looked like. Both families were fake and made up for entertainment purposes; however, it was what I saw, heard, and believed family should look like. It left a mental impression on my idea of marriage. The Evans were a poor family, living in the projects, making ends meet the best way they could. While they had disagreements, the show always ended with them resolving issues, making up, and moving on like a big happy family. The Huxtables were more of the upper-class family; their show also ended with them resolving issues and moving on as a big happy family.

Nevertheless, as much as I loved both of those shows, they gave me a false perception of marriage. I also grew up in the church and around couples that were married. The family would come to church dressed in their Sunday's best clothes. Everybody sat together, they would praise and worship together, smiling as if everything was good. You never saw or heard of the family being in distress or having issues. From the outside looking in, being married with children looked easy, happy, and darn good! My question is who or what gave you your first perception of marriage? Rather it was through television, the church, or you were raised in a two-parent home, I can almost guarantee what you saw is what you thought marriage would be for you, rather good or bad, it left a mental impression. Unknowingly, we carry those impressions into our marriage. I have never been divorced, but I have counseled people who have gone through divorce. The clear majority did not go through deliverance before entering their next relationship and/or marriage. Divorce can also leave a mental impression of many false perceptions that without deliverance you will carry over with you into your next relationship. Again, moving on does not equate to deliverance.

The false perception that almost destroyed my marriage was believing marriage was going to fix the flaws in our relationship. I thought marriage would fix me and him. I thought, if we got married, surely God would bless us, and all our problems would magically disappear. If we got married, the past ungodly soul ties would immediately be broken, and the residue of sexual immorality would be gone from the both of us. Financial instability would stabilize itself. If not, then surely, we would be able to resolve every issue and move on as a happy family. And, when this did not happen, I began looking at other marriages and started comparing my marriage with others. I would compare Reggie to other married men. I made sure to point out to him the good in everybody else's husband, the good in everybody else's marriage. Little did I know I had bought into the false perception of marriage.

Trust and believe there are consequences to believing in false perceptions. Once you believe the lie, you build upon the lie! The false perception has now become your reality and your reality is a lie! You will spend years trying to hold the lie together, so your marriage looks good from the outside. We did this for years! And it cost us dearly. Not only us but our children as well. Do not be deceived into thinking your children are exempt from reaping the effects of your false perception when they are forced to live the lie. While you think you are protecting them from your lies and secrets, they have become products of your lies and nine times out of ten become little liars themselves. You have introduced them to the spirit of secretism and a generational curse that cannot be beat or punished out of them.

So, the way to dispel your false perception of marriage is to deal with the true perception of marriage. What is the true perception of marriage? It is a submission to oneness! I know it sounds too simple to be true. And let me tell you, it is easier said than done. Ephesians 5:22-33 is the scripture Christian marriages build their foundation on. It has been titled the "Analogy of Marriage," but if I could retitle it, I would change it to the "Analogy of Deliverance for Marriage." I can vividly remember this

THE ANALOGY OF DELIVERANCE FOR MARRIAGE!

Ephesians 5:22-33

scripture being the core scripture of our pre-martial counseling and no disrespect to the Pastor that took us through pre-martial counseling, but DELIVERANCE was never mentioned or pointed out to us during our process. Submission to oneness was never discussed. And we take full responsibility for our lack of knowledge and understanding of the Word at that time. Marriage is a beautiful thing! Covenant is beautiful! Love is beautiful! Family is beautiful! The path to this beauty will lead you to the end of yourself. It will lead you to deliverance. Submission to oneness is the action of accepting and yielding to the will of God and the will of your spouse, to bring forth a unified force that cannot be penetrated by man, woman, or darkness. As the wife submits to her husband, the husband submits to the authority of Christ as the head of the family. And this action gives birth to ONENESS!

Submission **gives birth to ONENESS!**

It was through deliverance oneness was birthed into our marriage. It was a hard process. We both were a piece of work. Once Reggie submitted to the authority of Christ and I saw this, I was able to submit to my deliverance process and submit to be his wife. I did not go into my marriage submitted to my husband because my husband was not submitted to the authority of Christ. Once he submitted to the authority of Christ, I had to step back and get in my rightful place alongside of him and not in front of him trying to lead and control the dynamics of our marriage. I still have to fall back! That is a continual deliverance process for me. When I want to fix things and take lead, I hear the Holy Spirit loud and clear telling me to FALL BACK! I had to understand when I get out of order it brings division, chaos, and confusion. It goes against oneness. Reggie had to understand that he could not lead me or this family without submitting to the authority of Christ. And brothers let me tell you going to church every Sunday does not mean you have submitted to the authority of Christ. Going through deliverance does! Reggie will testify, the process of true deliverance was difficult, but it was what helped make him understand what submitting to the authority of Christ truly meant. He struggled with rejection, lust, masturbation, pornography, perversion, infidelity, alcoholism, pride, filthy lucre, dishonesty, and secretism. All of these kept him from leading his family by the authority of Christ. You see, we both had our own needs of deliverance. Once we went through self-deliverance our marriage went through complete deliverance and is still going through deliverance. It is an ongoing process that we must submit to daily.

Do not go into your marriage or if you are married, do not believe the false perception that your marriage will not go through some hard times. Do not believe the false perception that you are so holy, so right, so good, so great, and so powerful, that you will not need to go through deliverance at every new stage your marriage graduates too. Remember, while you are fighting to stay in covenant and stay in oneness, Satan is fighting against your covenant and against your oneness! With some of his fights he has been given legal rights due to some of your bad choices and sinful habits.

Deliverance for My Soul and My Marriage

Once lies and false perception has lodged into your soul it contaminates your mental impression, allowing sin to enter your mind, heart, and soul. Deliverance is necessary! As I stated earlier, sin gives the enemy legal rights to torment and wreak havoc on your life and marriage. To revoke his legal rights, you must repent and go through deliverance. Complete deliverance! What does complete deliverance look like? Complete deliverance is bringing your spirit, soul, and body into alignment with the Word of God. All three parts! **I Thessalonians 5:23** says, ***"And the very God of peace sanctify you wholly; and I pray God your whole spirit and soul and body be preserved blameless unto the coming of our Lord Jesus Christ."*** Deliverance is the act of separating your soul from darkness and the entanglement of sin, addressing habitual manifestation and root causes of oppression, and bringing your soul back into its original state of freedom.

You will never be delivered from something you never recognize as a deliverance need. There were a lot of things I refused to acknowledge as a deliverance need. I would use the excuses of this is just the way I am, this is just me, I was born this way, I have been like this all my life, and I am not changing for nobody. This was the spirit of rebellion speaking. The mental bed was my bed of deliverance. I had my second mental breakdown at the age of thirty-seven. While I was in the mental hospital, the spirit of the Lord ministered to me so powerfully. As the reality hit me that I had attempted to take my life for the second time, I begin to call on the name of Jesus. Now at this time it was hard for me to determine what was real or what my mind had determined to be real. The doctors would call this hallucination because of the number of pills I had taken. I know now that it was all real! I was at my weakest and all I could mustard was a cry of JESUS! JESUS! JESUS! My heart hurt so bad I thought I was having a heart attack. Suddenly, the spirit of God began to assure me that I was going to be okay and that my marriage was going to survive this devastation. He asked me if I would let him put my broken pieces back together? If I would let him heal and deliver me? If I would let him help me? If I would let him save and deliver my marriage? At first, I was confused because I was thinking, you are God you can do whatever you want, so I never answered. The same questions kept being asked, repeatedly. Every time, I would dose off to sleep I would be taken back to certain events in my life going all the way back to my childhood. And when I would wake up, the spirit of the Lord was still hovering over me repeating the same questions. It was as if time had stood still because it seemed as this was going on for days. When I would wake up after each vision, I would realize only minutes had ticked off the clock and not hours or days. In my mind I was saying no! I am ashamed and embarrassed I can never stay in this marriage; it had gone beyond saving. I would not speak it though I was only thinking it.

During each event of my past that I revisited, I could see from a distance how God was in it, protecting me. And again, the same questions: will you let me heal you? Will you let me save your marriage? Will you let me deliver you and your marriage? Finally, I opened my mouth and a "YES!" roared out of me! And all of a sudden, I began to feel this overwhelming feeling of compassion and love for Reggie. I was confused because I wanted to hate him and be mad at him, but my heart would not let me. My mind was saying hate, but my heart was saying love. Love began to put me back together, love began to minister to me, love began to calm me, love began to heal me. God began to show me how all of those hurtful events had grown me into a giant! That night my prayers turned into prayers of deliverance. It was in that moment I realized that I had never gone through deliverance. My perception of deliverance at that time was purging and spitting up demons or some type of demonic manifestation. I did not think I had demons attached to me because I was going to church and I thought I was saved. I cried all night as I reflected on how I had been playing Russian Roulette with my salvation, my marriage, and my life. It was at that time I realized I had to deal with the truth of my life and my marriage. I could no longer hide behind the false perception. It was time for this giant to become a giant slayer and slay every demonic influence and close every demonic door that I had opened over my life and marriage. I recognized I had a serious deliverance need, playing church and living a lie was no longer an option for me. I did not wait for Reggie to come to the knowledge that he also needed deliverance or needed to submit to the authority of Christ. As a matter of fact, I stopped pointing out his faults, his dirt, his sins, and I started pointing that finger at myself. Little did I know the power of deliverance had also hit Reggie's spirit. Here he was thinking he was just helping me heal and helping me through my process when the power of deliverance began to invade his space. He started going through his own process of deliverance.

The beauty of individual deliverance was it was healing our marriage at the same time. We started confessing our faults and struggles to each other. Things we had never shared with each other the entire thirteen years we had been together. We repented to God and to each other. Cleaning up ourselves cleaned up our marriage! Yes, it was a process that took a few years. We accepted that it would not happen overnight, in a few weeks, or a few months. We had now been married for nine years, together for thirteen years in complete turmoil, chaos, confusion, and self-destruction. But we knew God was the redeemer of time and if we committed to the process, behold he would make all things new. This process began to paint a beautiful picture of what marriage and oneness should look like and we quickly realized our marriage had purpose. To this day, we are still being delivered! At every stage our marriage graduates to, we go through some sort of deliverance. The moment you think your marriage has arrived and no longer needs deliverance is the moment you get stuck. Do not get stuck at your last deliverance. I tell people all the time you are only as powerful as your last deliverance. Your marriage is only as strong as your last deliverance. Never stop seeking deliverance. Deliverance produces maturity and growth. Keep maturing and growing together!

PRAYER

Heavenly Father, I thank you that you are the redeemer of time! Redeem the time and everything I have lost in my marriage. Release the angel of strength to help me during my deliverance process. Remove every lie that has lodged into my soul and release the spirit of Truth. I rebuke every demonic imprint of false perception that has affected my mind, will, and emotions and release the mind of Christ according to Philippians 2:5 over the door post of my mind. Teach me how to cast down vain imagination and everything that exhalteth itself over the knowledge of God. Holy Spirit, identify every false perception and uproot them with the sword of truth. Bring forth deliverance and healing in my marriage so that the true purpose of my marriage can be manifested in the earth. I surrender and invite you into those areas I never dealt with prior to my marriage. Let deliverance come forth in every season of my marriage from this day forth, I submit to the ongoing process from glory to glory. I ask for your wisdom and guidance through this process. Fill me with your Holy Spirit, your love, your peace, and your worship! Break every curse I have knowingly and unknowingly spoken over my marriage out of ignorance and frustration. I decree and declare my marriage is blessed, my marriage is healed, my marriage is delivered, my marriage is whole and my marriage is an everlasting covenant until death. Let me have patience to see this process through to the end. Heavenly Father, I ask that you restore my marriage and every martial covenant I am connected to through family and friendships. In Jesus Name!

JOURNAL

Your Thoughts & Notes From This Chapter

Chapter Five

FAMILY SECRETS, THE SILENT KILLER

"I feel bare, I didn't realize I wore my secrets as armor until they were gone and now everyone sees me as I really am."
~Veronica Roth~

What goes on in this house, stays in this house is a lie straight from hell! I do not know who started this saying, but this cliché has destroyed families and has now taken on the form of a generational curse that has been passed on from generation to generation. Somehow many of us have been taught to lie and pretend for the sake of looking good to the natural eyes of others. It was frowned upon to tell the truth of what was going on inside the home and through the family blood line. As a matter of fact, if you told anybody what was really going on you would be in serious trouble! Reggie and I did not realize we were birthed into families of secretism, dysfunction, and chaos until it spilled over into our relationship and marriage. My prayer is that by the end of this chapter, every plot, scheme, and plan of the enemy to contaminate your family bloodline through lies, deceit, dishonesty, and secrets will be exposed and destroyed. May the arrows of deliverance be released through your bloodline, with the fire of God on the tip of every arrow to destroy generations of lies, deceit, and secrets. May family secrets be revealed and exposed to bring about clarity, truth, peace, healing, and deliverance to the now generation and the generations to come.

Spirit of Secretism

The spirit of secretism wants to remain hidden and unexposed to Believers and families. I had to do some deep research to find the core of this spirit and for the sake of simplicity, I will expose only what the Holy Spirit has released me to write. There were not a lot of Christian teachings on this spirit. I searched every deliverance book I have including the demon dictionary and I could not find one teaching or background on this spirit. I was shocked and then the Holy Spirit reminded me why. The power of the spirit of secretism is ignorance and lack of knowledge and it wants to remain hidden. The less we know about this spirit, the more power we give it from generation to generation. Therefore, with the grace of God, I went onto the dark side to get the information I needed. Before you tune me out let me say this: the power that you need to understand and defeat this spirit is knowledge. Why is it Satan can step into our world/life and learn everything he needs to know about us, but we are afraid to do the same? Well, I am not afraid, here is what I found: The spirit of secretism is derived from the spirit of *mysteres* which is considered the dawn of the Dark Age, in the demonic realm. Secretism is the acting in a mysterious fashion; not giving full disclosure. It is a concealment of the truth, often rooted in fear, terror, and torment. The invocation of secrecy is to restrict the flow of truthful information. It is a controlling spirit with a hidden agenda to divide, deteriorate relationships, and silence truth with a long history of excessive lies and chaos.

SCRIPTURES:

Revelation 12:11— *" And they overcame him (Satan), by the blood of the Lamb, and by the word of their testimony; and they loved not their lives unto the death."*

Proverbs 28:13— *"He who conceals his transgressions will not prosper, But he who confesses and forsakes them will find compassion"*

Psalms 90:8—	*"You have placed our iniquities before You, Our secret sins in the light of Your presence."*
Psalms 19:12—	*"Who can discern his errors? Acquit me of hidden faults."*
Isaiah 29:15—	*"Woe to those who deeply hide their plans from the LORD, and whose deeds are done in a dark place, And they say, "Who sees us?" or "Who knows us?"*
John 3:20—	*"For everyone who does evil hates the Light and does not come to the Light for fear that his deeds will be exposed.*
Ephesians 5:11—	*"Do not participate in the unfruitful deeds of darkness, but instead even expose them.*

The first thing I want to point out is the Dark Age is also referred to as "Era of Darkness" (from a.d. 476 to about 1000), the middle age period which was marked by ignorance and the lack of advanced knowledge. It was a state of stagnation and decline. It was a period where records during this time were lost and/or hidden until this present day. There is no surprise the spirit of secretism is an ancient spirit that travels through the bloodline from generation to generation in attempts to bring ages of darkness, chaos, and confusion to families, operating as a silent killer. Essentially, the spirit of secretism produces years of dysfunctional relationships. The spirit of secretism is masterfully a silent killer because it works as the python spirit, quietly squeezing the life out of you by keeping your mouth shut from telling the truth. The more it squeezes, the more fearful you become. The more it squeezes, the more tormented you become. Most time causing a slow death, both physically and spiritually. It amazes me the great lengths we will go through to protect a lie and to keep the truth from coming out, especially when the lie involves family secrets.

Secrets that are traumatic, painful, or life-changing can damage an entire generation. It can cause the next generation and the next generation to be birthed and developed into a generation of witchcraft, lies, division, chaos, confusion, anger, bitterness, unforgiveness, fear, and torment that can cause major damage. It can produce a lineage of mental issues, emotional issues, a history of family infirmities, and a history of dysfunction. If you find a repeated cycle in your family bloodline like reoccurring infirmities (high blood pressure, diabetes, heart disease, kidney disease, cancer, addiction, migraines, digestive problems, depression, bipolar, and/or mental health issues and/or a repeated cycle of molestation, incest, rape, perversion, lying, then the demonic has been given legal rights to your family bloodline through the spirit of secretism).

As a child, my family history was never discussed. I did not know much about my mother, grandmother, or great grandmother's life. It was never talked about. I do not ever recall being told about my grandfather or great grandfather. There is so much confusion and dysfunction in my mom's family bloodline due to family secrets, my generation is still trying to figure out what is true, whose child is who's due to molestation, incest, and sexual abuse. It is a mess! Our ancestors took their secrets to the grave with them, leaving a legacy of division, dysfunction, loss identity, chaos, and confusion.

I am a product of a 42-year family secret. One day my mom and I were on the phone having a conversation about all our family secrets. It was the first time I had ever heard my mom mentioned certain things (not good) about our family. Out of the 42 years of my life and the many conversations we have had, suddenly, she was releasing all the families best kept secrets. I began to say to her how sad it was for my grandmother and great grandmother to carry all those secrets to the grave with them and now I understood why the family was so divided. In her silence, I was led to ask her if there were any secrets she needed to release and not carry to the grave with her. After a very long pause, she responded with a "yes, there is one concerning you, but I rather tell you face to face," she said. "Oh, no Lady Bug, you have had 42 years and plenty of face to faces with me. You can tell me now and we can talk about it face to face," I said. And I was not getting off that phone until she told me. Finally, she said, "Butch, is not your biological father. A man name Albert Goodson is your real father. I was young, in my teens pregnant with my second child. Mama was already raising Trevas and I knew she would be pissed with me being pregnant again. Albert was young, handsome, and a lady's man. When I told him I was pregnant, he did not believe me and brushed me off with a 'from who?' Devastated by his response, I slept with Butch and told him I was pregnant. His response was pure joy, let's get married.

And that is what I did. I married him, and you became his child." Although shocked, I was not surprised.

Subsequently, at the age of 15, I began to struggle with depression and suicidal thoughts. I had never had a father-daughter relationship with my father (Butch). I always knew who he was, but he was not present in my life growing up. I had a stepfather that I was close to, but all of a sudden, I was having this great desire to have a relationship with my father. It was a real struggle for me, not understanding where all these emotions were coming from. One day I was having one of my depressed moments crying and crying wanting to know why I could not have a relationship with my father. Why he did not love me enough to call me or come see me whenever I would go to his mom's house after church hoping and praying to see him? Wondering why I never got a Happy Birthday or a Christmas gift from him? Out of nowhere a voice spoke to me and told me to stop crying. He is not your father. A calm and peace came over me in that moment. I did not ask questions or try to figure out where the voice came from. In that moment, there was a sense of truth and I immediately knew it was true.

The next day my mom and I were riding in the car and I said to her, "You know Butch is not my father." I had a smile on my face because finally it made sense to me and I did not have to feel unwanted anymore. My mom became very angry and asked, "Who told you that!" I responded, "Nobody told me. I just know because a voice told me." My mom was livid with me and went through great lengths to protect her secret. She took me to the youth counselor at our church and I was made to believe that demons were talking to me, that the voice that I heard was not real, and that I was being rebellious. This confused me even more and made me angry because I knew what I had heard. And as crazy as they thought I was, hearing he was not my father at that time brought peace to my mind and soul. It was easier for me to accept he was not my father than to accept the feeling of rejection, unwantedness, and abandonment from him. This experience opened a wound and the suicidal thoughts and bouts of depression increased. Now my anger was directed towards my mom for embarrassing me and telling the people at church I was hearing and talking to demons. I developed a strong love/hate feeling towards her. I loved her because she was my mom, but I hated her for what she had done. It was not long after that experience that I acted on the suicidal thoughts and almost succeeded. I was in ICU for two days and spent a week in the hospital and one month in a mental/behavioral treatment facility. I went through all of that, so my mom could protect her secret. I almost died, and it still took my mom twenty-six more years to confess her secret. For years our relationship suffered and was in complete turmoil. Her secret was my silent killer! Her silence produced years of hurt, pain, depression, dysfunction, rejection, unwantedness, abandonment, anger, hate, rebellion, and mental issues. Her moment of truth was another level of deliverance for me because now it all made sense and I was not crazy after all. While I had gone through deliverance by the time she told me, and our relationship had been restored to a loving and respectable place, it still took me three years to process my truth and I am still processing it.

I encourage you to bring freedom and deliverance to your bloodline by exposing every lie and every secret. Tell your children the truth! You may think you are protecting them by not telling them the truth, but I am a living witness that your silence becomes their silent killer. My greatest deliverance came by telling my daughter everything I had done in my past. During this conversation, I found out that she too was now struggling with the exact same things as I had. It was the first time I began to study and research generational curses. Generational curses are birthed and established through the spirit of secretism. James 5:16 (a) says: "Confess your faults one to another, and pray one for another, that ye may be healed." It does not say keep silent about your faults. You overcome this spirit and break it off your blood line by the word of your testimony, the blood of Jesus, and loving not the lie until death. Say yes to truth. Become vulnerable to your truth and align every lie, every secret, and every scheme with the Word of God.

Heavenly Father, sprinkle the blood of Jesus over my family blood line! Expose every family secret. I bind the spirit of secretism and break it off my bloodline going back 100 generations. I bind every spirit that is attached to this spirit—lying, infirmities, sickness and disease, deceit, sexual impurities, incest, molestation, rape, anger, hate, mental illness, dysfunction, and division. May every spirit be uprooted and casted out of my bloodline. I decree that I will be the voice of truth in my family and will expose every lie of the enemy that has tried to remain hidden in my family. I bind family secrets, in the name of Jesus! Jehovah Gibbor fight for my family! Deliver my family from every lie, every secret, and every hidden thing. Release Your fire and burn up the works of darkness according to Psalm 140:10: Let burning coals fall upon every secret: let every secret be cast into the fire; into deep pits that they rise not up again! Close up the breach that would give Satan and demons access to my family in the name of Jesus. I stand in the gap for my family and make up the hedge of protection for the generations to come, now and forever! Bind up all breaches, O Lord and let the walls of truth and salvation be raised over my family and over my seed from generation to generation. I bind and cast out all spirits of guilt, condemnation, unworthiness, shame, and embarrassment in the name of Jesus Christ! I break and release my family from all generational curses and iniquities as a result of the secret sins of our ancestors. I break every time-released curse that may try to activate in my generation and the generations to come. Let every legal right be revoked NOW in Jesus name! Lord release your power and spirit over the _____ (family name) bloodline. Release your love, unity, and wisdom over us and loose us into your marvelous truth and light. I pray this prayer by faith,

In Jesus name!

JOURNAL

Your Thoughts & Notes From This Chapter

Chapter Six

FORGIVING THE UNFORGIVABLE

"They caused the first wound, but you are causing the rest; this is what not forgiving does. They got it started, but you keep it going. Forgive and let it go, or it will eat you alive. You think they made you feel this way, but when you won't forgive, you are the one inflicting the pain on yourself."
~Bryant McGill~

When the Holy Spirit gave me the title of this chapter, I thought it was a contradiction to mention forgiving and unforgivable in the same line. I thought to myself, Holy Spirit you have to teach this one. And He reminded me that He had already taught it to me, through my life experiences. Forgiveness is one of the foundations of Christian biblical teachings, yet unforgiveness is the number one killer of marriages and relationships. Why is the divorce rate the highest in the body of believers verses non-believers? I believe it is because we are only being taught forgiveness through the eyes of Christ and not as the nature of Christ. Taught through the eyes of man, but not as the nature of man. Most definitely, we know what forgiveness means. Biblically, we know what forgiveness means, but we have failed to take on the nature of forgiveness. We have spoken the words "I forgive you," but we do not have the characteristics of "I forgive you." We think we get to pick and choose what forgiveness looks like within our marriage. What we should and should not forgive. What we can and cannot forgive. I ask you to read this chapter with an open heart in order to hear my heart and understand my desire for you to take on the nature of Christ through forgiveness. True Forgiveness!

I am sure if you are reading this by now you have heard many teachings and preached sermons on forgiveness. You probably know and can quote scriptures on forgiveness, just as I can. Therefore, I decided to take the literal approach on forgiveness, which will tie into every scripture you have probably read on forgiveness. I honestly thought I was a forgiving person and had a clear understanding of what forgiveness was, until I was faced with the ultimate betrayal within my marriage and I realized that I did not understand forgiveness and had not forgiven a lot of past hurts, issues, and problems not just within my marriage but throughout my life experiences. I had this false perception of forgiveness. I thought because I had been in relationship with my husband for many years that I had forgiven him for all past hurts, disagreements, arguments, and disappointments. During this process I quickly realized that I had not forgiven and was holding onto every offense. I had moved on, but I had not forgiven. Things from my childhood, adulthood, past relationships, were all suppressed in my heart, causing me to be an emotional wreck. I was so unstable in my emotions. I was a ticking time bomb. Anything would set me off! But I never equated my behavior to unforgiveness. I never equated my bad attitude, anger, and hardened heart to unforgiveness. You want to know what came along and knocked me off my high horse. My sweet, loving, "lawd I want to be married" HUSBAND, in the form of the Holy Spirit. I know that sounds crazy and believe me I thought it was, especially when I was going through it! I told you earlier marriage is DELIVERANCE!

My process started in 2006. I used to lead this song in the choir called "Calling My Name" by Hezekiah Walker. Although I had led this song many times before, on this one particular Sunday something different happened to me as I sung this song. There was a breaking! At that time, my life was in total chaos. I was in a bisexual relationship and still married to my husband. I think my husband knew the relationship with this female was more than just a friendship, but he was so caught up in his own lies and deceit that it really did not matter to him, as long as he had a piece of me, he was good. The words to the following song are (read carefully):

How many times, do I go against Your will

Then You forgive me, but yet I still

Turn around and do the things, the things I shouldn't do

Cause I belong to You and I know You will come through

Lord I know, I take advantage of Your grace

Here in this Christian race,

But yet I still hear You calling my name

How many times, would it take for me to learn

That it's only in Your will, I'll ever earn

I'll ever earn my life's reward, the honor due to me

Life eternally, riches in Glory

Lord, I know, I know I don't belong

With You cause I've done wrong

But yet I still hear You calling my name

You're calling my name to come into Your arms

To be safe from fear and harm.
Knowing this but I still choose to go my way
And You still say, You say that I am He
Who will supply your every need
Oh Lord I sinned but You're still calling my name

Powerful right? How can I expect to keep leading this song and repeating those words without God showing up? After leading this song many, many times one Sunday, for the first time, I heard the words to this song. Meaning, the words to the song finally found me and ministered to me! All the times before this song ministered to other people, but not me. That night while lying in bed I heard my spirit man singing *"Oh, Lord I sinned, but you're still calling my name"* over and over again, the same line *"Oh, Lord I sinned, but you're still calling my name."* I remember thinking, but I am not ready to answer the call. I have too much going on (sin) in my life and I was not ready to give it all up. I did not realize the demonic realm I had tapped into by my lifestyle and the choices I was making. God knew he had to show me and that is exactly what he did! The very next weekend I was with my female lover and during intimacy, out of nowhere she turned into a demon. It was her but what I saw was a demon, it had the facial shape of a rat with horns and small sharp teeth. I could see it slowly sucking the life out of me. I could see pieces of my soul being extracted from my body through this demon. It was as if everything had slowed down to a speed that I could see what was going on. I could hear a voice saying, "Now you see?" I was not afraid and that was strange to me because most people fear demons, but not me, I was calm, like, "okay, I see you." I got up and immediately left! In the car ride home, I cried and prayed. I asked God to forgive me and made a vow that I would stop all my infidelity and would be faithful to Him and my husband. And I did. What I did not know was that because of my obedience, deliverance was about to hit my entire house!

Exposure

There cannot be deliverance or forgiveness without exposure! At some point, you will have to deal with the truth! In 2007, after being clean and walking a straight line for over a year, exposure hit my home. One of the biggest misconceptions is once you Repent and turn from your wicked ways, it cancels the consequences. Repentance only extends grace for you to be sustained through the reaping of your harvest. Galatians 6:7 says: "Do not be deceived: God cannot be mocked. A man reaps what he sows."

March 2007, after hearing rumors for a few years that Reggie had conceived a child outside of our marriage was confirmed to be true. As strong as I thought I was nothing could prepare me for the pain, disappointment, and embarrassment that consumed me in a matter of minutes. Even in the midst of the chaos God was with me. Please believe me, it was CHAOTIC! I think I fought him until I almost passed out. He was crying, I was crying, biting, scratching, hitting, kicking, and yelling, just a wave of emotions. After all the fighting, I began to settle into what was going on and I tried to wrap my mind around it all. I was introduced to spirit of betrayal. It was so overwhelming it consumed my mind, will, and emotions. If you have never dealt with betrayal the best way I can describe it is a feeling of complete sadness and emptiness. It was like diving into a bottomless pit of darkness. I could see no end to the pain. How could someone I loved so deeply deceive me so well? But in that moment, all I wanted was his love. I battled with still loving him in that moment. I told him to get out and as he was taking his clothes out of the closet, I began to put them back in the closet. Again, I was having one of those out of body experiences. Standing back watched myself put his clothes back in the closet confused at love. Hating love, hating myself for loving him, hating him, not loving him—I was so confused and hurt. The weird part was I could also feel Reggie's hurt, pain, and embarrassment. I remember telling him, I can feel your pain and my pain, and it is just too much for me to bare! I had crazy dreams that night. I could feel the demonic realm trying to get access to me. I would wake up feeling like I was falling and trying to catch myself. I was searching for an end to the pain and could not find one. Each time I dozed off to sleep I would fall deeper into this darkness, but I was fighting to stop falling. I would get weaker and weaker and finally, I gave up the fight.

The next morning, I woke up to a familiar feeling of darkness and sadness. I knew I was going to commit suicide. No second thoughts, I just knew. I went downstairs got a beer out the fridge and my Ambien sleeping pills. As soon as I got back in the bed, the demon appeared. I immediately knew who he was. I greeted him with "Hey, I know who you are." He confirmed, "Yes, you met me when you were 16 years old. I helped you then and I am here to help you again." (PAUSE: I am not crazy, this happened for real. If you do not think demons are real, I am here to tell you, they are very much real!) The suicide demon appears as a false agent of light. It appears to be friendly and very nice. It tells you all the reasons why you should take your life and how you are going to a much better place. How the people around you will be better off without you and they would want you to take your life. It is the total opposite of what you imagine demons to be (scary and evil). The demon was helping in feeding me the pills and as I would try to stop, it would then become aggressive and eager to complete its assignment. You still have a conscience to know it is wrong, yet you are unable to stop it once it takes control. Every time I hear someone has succeeded in committing suicide my heart breaks because I know exactly what they went through. While other people try to make sense out of it, I completely understand. I do not remember much after taking the pills. I do remember seeing demons coming out of my closet trying to get to me. I saw the hedge of protection around me, preventing them from getting to me. They could not touch my bed! Everybody said when I came too, the first thing I told everyone about was the demons and how they were trying to get to me and God would not let them. I do not remember telling them this. It was all a blur to me. I finally regained consciousness later that night and was told I would be going to the mental hospital. As I stated earlier, the mental bed was my bed of deliverance.

The next day Reggie came to the mental hospital to see me; and it was his words to me that confirmed my marriage had purpose. I had not talked to him; therefore, he did not know my mental state or about my dreams and visitation from the Holy Spirit the night before. As I shared earlier, the Holy Spirit ministered to me so powerfully the night before that when I saw Reggie all my anger and hate for him was now this overwhelming feeling of compassion and mercy. We greeted each other with a LONG embrace and tears. I was speechless, so he spoke first, and he said something so simple but changed my entire mental state. He said, "Let me help you through this. I caused this pain and just let me help you through this and if you decide to divorce me after you get better; I will understand and agree. Let's not make this about if we are going to get a divorce but about you getting healed." I was expecting him to come in begging me to forgive him and stay with him and to make it all about him. Instead, he asked to help me through my process. It was at that moment, for the first time in our marriage, my spirit connected to his spirit and we both realized how much we needed each other.

After years of chaos, confusion, and dysfunction we finally decided to go through marriage counseling. We both decided that secular counseling would work best for us. At that time, we did not have or trust anyone to take us through spiritual counseling. But God was still working behind the scenes. We selected a name off our insurance plan website. The Doctor we selected turned out to be a Believer. We went through six months of counseling together and individually. Now for me, my process was more detailed because of my past experiences with attempted suicide. This time I had someone who believed and understood demons are real and did not write me off as being crazy or having mental issues. She did not give me spiritual counseling, but she recommended I seek God regarding my faith and ask him to connect me to a spiritual leader that would help me get the spiritual help I needed. What she did not know and what I did not remember was Reggie had gotten to the house just as the paramedics were taking me out of the house and I came through for a second and told Reggie to call Pastor Lott. I absolutely do not remember this. That call lead us to "True Worship Christian Center" were we both joined and got "saved" for real! And our deliverance process began.

True Forgiveness

In the year of 2010, we had now been going through the process of rebuilding the foundation of our marriage for three years now. We were both leaders in our new church. I had gone through some serious deliverance. I was committed and a bit selfish during my process. I was determined that nobody (husband, children, myself, or mom) was ever going to break me to the point of suicide again. My strength and foundation were going to be rooted and grounded in God and God alone. For the first time in my life I focused on my inner man and inner healing. I begin to change to the point that it scared my family! Prayer and studying the Word of God became my life. I had since been appointed as the praise and worship leader and began to flow in the prophetic. Here comes my test. February 2010, we had an all-night prayer at the church. My appointed time to pray over the atmosphere was 2:00 a.m. right before the witching hour (3:00 a.m.). During my prayer the Holy Spirit led me to pray over my marriage. I remember asking God to expose every hidden thing and to remove every stumbling block. I began to war in the spirit like I had never done before! My heavenly language hit a realm in the spirit that shook me and the entire atmosphere.

We got home and immediately went to bed because we had been up all night. I begin to hear Reggie's phone vibrate back to back. Since he was in a deep sleep, I answered his phone. I woke him up and gave him the phone. When I asked who the female was, he tried to down-play it. I am bad with remembering phone numbers, but I somehow remembered this number. I left the house a few hours later headed to a funeral and called the number back and spoke with the young lady who verified she was having an affair with my husband. She began to cry on the phone and I began to pray with her that God would heal her broken heart and give her strength. Yes, after hearing this woman is sleeping with my husband, I prayed with her. I could not believe the compassion I felt for her. She was brought to more tears as I prayed with her and told me she could not believe that I had just prayed with her so powerfully after hearing she was sleeping with my husband. I told her it was not me, but it was all God! When I got home I advised Reggie I had spoken with her and knew the truth. I will never forget the look on his face. He was waiting for me to act a fool, you know the look when you know you are about to fight (yeah that look). I told him, "You better go get on your face and repent to God before you even think about talking to me. You sinned against God and you still playing with your salvation." He quickly took my advice and locked himself in a room and I could hear him crying and praying to God.

    I am not sure if he was thanking God for saving him from me, because I am pretty sure by the look in his eyes, his mind went back to the last time I found out he was cheating. To be honest, I shocked myself. I was not sure what I was going to do regarding staying in my marriage or divorcing him, but I knew I was not going to make a move until I heard from God. By now, it was clear to me Reggie was dealing with a demonic stronghold. I told him he would have to sleep on the couch until I heard from God as to what to do about our marriage and his continued infidelity. I did not want or need his apology. I wanted him to be delivered! God did not answer me that day or the next day. So, I prayed and told God if it was His will for me to stay in my marriage, I would have to see with my own eyes that demon casted out! Three weeks had gone by and nothing. Apostle Fannie Wallace and her apostolic team were coming for a three day conference at our church. She requested to have a meeting with Reggie and I while she was in town. The meeting was scheduled for that Saturday, late afternoon. I was prepared to tell Reggie in that meeting that I wanted a divorce.

Friday night service was powerful! I was leading praise and worship, I was in a zone. I heard the Holy Spirit tell me to open my eyes. When I did in a distance I could see Pastor JT and Prophetess Natalie on the ground with somebody. I realized it was Reggie. I stopped singing and stood there frozen because nobody knew what I had said to God but me and him! I watched my husband's deliverance and saw that demon be cast out of him! If you have ever gone through deliverance you know it drains you when demonic spirits are being casted out because it is literally a war for your soul taking place. Once Reggie came to, he began to crawl to me because he was too weak to stand and walk. When we embraced, instant healing took place. The next day we met with Apostle Fannie and I began to tell her of the events that had taken place over the last few weeks and the past three years back to my suicide attempt. Her words that day changed my life forever! She asked me if I had forgiven Reggie. I thought she was talking about the recent incident. She said NO for the affair that birthed kids outside of your marriage. Well surely, I had forgiven him because I was still with him. She told me just because you stayed with him does not mean you forgave him. She looked at Reggie and asked him if I still bring it up when we get into a disagreement? He responded nodding his head slowly to say yes. She looked at me and told me I had not forgiven him and I did not understand "true forgiveness." She said, "If you keep bringing it up every time you get a chance, baby you have not forgiven him, and this marriage will never heal. True forgiveness is when you forgive your offender (your husband) and love them like it never happened! Him and her! And every time the enemy tries to bring it back to your remembrance, remind that joker that since God has forgiven them, so have you! You are working with the enemy when you do this because he is the only one that tries to hold you in bondage to your past."

Then she flipped the script on me! She told me I was good at telling his story and everything he had done wrong within the marriage. How about you tell me your story? What have you done? Have you cheated? Have you lied? Have you hurt him? A wave of emotions came over me as I thought back over where God had brought me and delivered me from. In that moment, I heard the Holy Spirit say, "The same grace." The Holy Spirit began to deal with me and I realized that Reggie also had not forgiven himself. How could he when I kept reminding him of his past instead of prophesying to his future, our future! The life of my marriage or the death of my marriage was in my tongue. I could forgive and speak life, or I could not forgive and speak death. Either way it was my choice (freedom of choice). I chose life! I took my husband by the hand and repented for joining in with Satan and his plan to hold him in bondage to his past. I said to him, "I forgive you, for real this time. However, this is your last get out of jail free card! If you can't be faithful to me, love me, desire only me and be in covenant with me and only me; divorce me! I am healed now. I promise you, I will be fine." I made him look me in my eyes and I told him if I had to share him with other women, I DID NOT want him and released him to go find that woman, because I was not her! I reiterated to him, "If I can't have all of you, I don't want none of you." I did not have to cuss, fight, or force love in that moment because this time my words had power. For the first time in my life my security was in God and not a man. True forgiveness helped love win and we have been winning since that day.

Your marriage can survive infidelity. It will not survive unforgiveness. True forgiveness will resurrect you, your spouse, and your marriage (to forgive and love your spouse like it never happened). Let me go on record and say forgiveness and trust are two different things and have two different meanings. Forgiveness does not automatically restore trust. You will have to put things in place to restore the trust. Trust is the strength of marriage and without it the marriage will be fragile. I let Reggie know off top, me forgiving you does not mean I trust you. Once we both understood that we put things in place that would help restore the trust. I have never seen Reggie work so hard to regain my trust. Once I released my husband from the bondage of my unforgiveness, it allowed his healing and deliverance process to go to the next level. This is exactly what our marriage needed. I needed him to love God more than he loved me! I wanted his security to be in God and not in his ability to smooth talk a woman into the bed with him. I knew that false sense of security would be the death of his prophetic future and our marriage.

Infidelity – Grounds for Divorce?

There is no doubt that sexual misconduct such as infidelity could be grounds for divorce. The magic word is could be, not must be. I know from experience that infidelity is one of the most painful situations to recovery from. So painful that many have found it impossible to recover from and move on in their marriage, leading to divorce.

In Matthew 19:3-12, Jesus is addressing this issue and he starts with reminding them of the foundation of marriage between male and female. For him to reiterate the foundational institution of marriage says to me that there had to be something going on during that time. I am not going to add to scripture, but I believe there is a strong reason why he emphasizes the foundation of marriage between a male and female. Basically, he is letting them know nothing has changed (or ever will change) about God's original plan and standard for marriage between one man and one woman. The Pharisees then asked him, "Why say unto him, why did Moses then command to give a writing of divorcement, and to put her away?" Jesus responded, ***"Because of the hardness of your hearts suffered you to put away your wives: but from the beginning it was NOT SO."*** The issue was not infidelity, it was unforgiveness! God's plan and standard is one man and one woman joined together in covenant dissolved only by death. This in no way gives free passes for infidelity. Marital unfaithfulness is a serious violation, especially repeated offenses, and God understands that more than we know because so are we. We are repeated offenders. How many times have we had to go back to him and ask for forgiveness for the same thing, repeatedly?

Do not get it twisted; I am in no way condoning infidelity, especially repeated infidelity. In fact, if the offender cannot or refuses to be faithful to his/her one spouse they should not be married. As I told my husband, "if you cannot be faithful to me; divorce me." There will be a consequence or consequences for your choice to commit adultery against God and your covenant. It may feel good in that moment, but it is going to cost you something! If you are reading this and you are a repeated offender of infidelity you must know there is a serious deliverance need to uproot the power you have given the enemy over you and your covenant. It is not your spouse's fault that you cannot be faithful, it is your own deliverance need. You must deal with you from a place of honesty and be willing to get to the root of your unfaithfulness and sexual immorality.

I understand forgiveness due to infidelity can be extremely difficult. The hurtful thoughts that keep creeping in your mind, keep you reliving the pain of the transgression. The thoughts of, "How can I forgive him/her? How can I forget this? How can I trust him/her again? How can I love someone that hurt me so bad? Will they do it again?" are difficult to overcome. Once you have experienced the pain associated with infidelity (betrayal, deceit, hurt, disappointment, anger, hate, rage, and fear) it will attempt to harden your heart immediately and put you on a dark path of unforgiveness. I will admit, it is one of the most painful experiences I have ever gone through. The first thing the enemy will do is try to make you think it is your fault and that something is wrong with you. (Warning: he will even use your spouse to put this weight on you). DO NOT fall for it! Your spouse's unfaithfulness is never about you so do not make it about you. The moment you make it about you it is a sign that your security is in a man/woman and not God. When your security is in God you realize that your spouse has sinned against God and the covenant; NOT you! When your security is truly in God, there is no room for the hardness of your heart (unforgiveness). I know you have probably heard time and time again that forgiveness is a process and it takes time to forgive. I hate to burst that religious bubble, but that is not scripture; it is a religious cliché.

Luke 17:4 says, *"And if he trespass against thee seven times a day, and seven times in a day returns again to thee, saying, I repent; thou shalt forgive him."* Nowhere in this scripture or any scripture does it say "Forgiveness is a process. Take your time and forgive when you are ready?

Only forgive if they trespass against you once?" Forgiving is an intentional action that is required of every believer. Be slow to judge and quick to forgive! You must be able to see pass the offense and if there is hope for true deliverance for your spouse, do not be so quick to walk away. I encourage you to make the decision to fight for your marriage or divorce from a healed and whole place; not from a bitter, revengeful, hurtful, resentful, and/or unforgiving place. Although you are not accountable for your spouse's action(s), you are responsible for your response(s) to their action(s). Nine times out of ten more damage is done to the marriage due to unforgiveness and the lack of resolved issues than the actual act of infidelity. It will take a commitment to deliverance (individual and maybe couples deliverance), inner healing, spiritual guidance, and/or counseling. **Your marriage can survive infidelity. It will not survive unforgiveness!**

Heavenly Father, I break the power of all witchcraft associated with the Judas spirit of betrayal, envy, strife, insecurities, comparison, and jealousy against my mind that causes confusion and fear. I plead the blood of Jesus over broken trust and the breach of covenant through infidelity and sexual immorality. I rebuke the demon of memory recall that attempts to invade my thoughts with negative thoughts of self- pity, shame, unforgiveness, retaliation, and undermining in the Mighty Name of Jesus. I forbid every trespassing negative thought from entering my soul that comes to cause damage to my emotions. Double-mindedness and delusion are bound up and removed from my life. I declare that I have the mind of Christ and the same mind that is in Christ Jesus is in me. I renounce the weight of heaviness, stress, bitterness, broken heart, pain, unforgiveness, and/or strife in my heart. I take off the garment of heaviness and arise with the garment of praise according to Isaiah 61:3. Lord, break up the fallow grounds in my heart; soften every hard place with your love and compassion. Create in me a clean heart and renew a right spirit in me, daily. I lay aside every weight and the sin which easily besets me and cast all my cares on you, Jesus. Deliver my marriage from the spirit of infidelity, deceit, dishonor, and secrets, expose every hidden thing. Every trespassing agent assigned to bring chaos, confusion, abuse, rejection, deception, and division to my marriage is cast out and commanded to return to its sender never to return to our bloodline again. I cancel your assignment and revoke your legal rights in the Mighty Name of Jesus. Every illegal soul tie is severed with the sword of the Spirit. The spirit of perversion and infidelity shall not destroy my marriage! I bind the spirit of divorce and reclaim the power of covenant agreement over my marriage. My marriage is bond in heaven and earth until death and the gate of hell shall not prevail against our covenant. I arm myself with the shield of faith to quench every fiery dart of the enemy aimed at my marriage. We repent for every spiritual breach and ask the Holy Spirit to seal every breach. I decree and declare that all layers of hurt and pain from the past are removed and replaced with the garment of healing and deliverance. I release the fruit of the spirit, love, peace, long-suffering, gentleness, goodness, faith, meekness, and temperance to flow in and through me and my spouse. I release the purity of love, unity, and an unbreakable bond that will stand against the covenant breaking spirit. I believe you can make all things new. I call forth the spirit of restoration and reconciliation. I decree my marriage is settled in the heavens now and forever. Thank you for hearing my prayer, in Jesus name!

JOURNAL

Your Thoughts & Notes From This Chapter

Chapter Seven

IS THERE ANYTHING TOO HARD FOR GOD?

Then came the word of the LORD unto Jeremiah, saying, Behold, I am the LORD, the God of all flesh: is there anything too hard for me?
Jeremiah 32:26-27

There is no doubt one of the greatest things God has given us in the earth realm is the martial covenant. It is the most powerful display of Oneness. More often than not, it takes you longer to come into agreement with heaven regarding your marriage, and your purpose/assignment in the earth realm. No matter how crazy it looks right now, your marriage has purpose in the earth. What I have found is that we fight harder against our destiny than the enemy. Our fleshly desires and pleasures of the world and our unbelief win most battles. A lot of us have been taught that every trial, tribulation, or issue that arises in life and/or marriages is an attack of the enemy. Instead of taking responsibility for our actions, we forget about the consequences of our choices and we blame the enemy. You will reap what you have sown and that is not spiritual warfare that is called reaping your harvest. The enemy cannot tear down what God has built and joined together. However, he can steal, kill, and destroy but only what you give him access to through sin including generational curses and disobedience. Once true repentance has taken place, grace steps onto the scene to help you deal with the consequences of your choices.

The only access the enemy has to you and your marriage is the legal access you and/or your spouse have given him through fleshly desires and pleasures of the world (sin). The real fight is against the flesh and not Satan! My prayer is as you read this chapter, you will gain strength to endure, your heart will be turned towards true repentance, you will gain the wisdom to rebuild and increased faith to know there is nothing too hard for God!

I will admit my faith in God concerning healing and deliverance for my marriage was a mental road block for a long time. Once exposure hit my marriage and the dirt, secrets, deceit, lies, and betrayal were revealed, I did not see my marriage being able to withstand the fortified places that we built (not the enemy); we did that! I could not see past the hurt and pain. I could not see past the guilt, shame, and embarrassment. I could not see God turning our mess into a miracle. My vision was blinded by doubt and unbelief. I really thought I believed in God until I was on the mental bed and the Holy Spirit kept asking me the same questions over and over again! I now know it was because of my unbelief. He kept asking because He knew I did not believe my marriage could be restored and that I could be delivered. He kept asking and taking me back to different time periods in my life until my faith increased to a YES! In that moment, doubt and unbelief was eradicated and God was able to begin the work.

The real work of restoration cannot begin until you uproot all doubt and unbelief. Let me ask you, "Is there anything too hard for God?" I know the natural response is no, there is nothing too hard for God. But what is your heart saying? You will know what your heart is speaking by your actions and by the words that come out of your mouth. What are you speaking and releasing over your marriage? What you speak is what you will get. Do you believe your marriage can be healed and delivered? Do you believe in the hope of your calling and the purpose of your marriage? Do you believe God has chosen you? Do you believe God can deliver you to a whole and healed place in Him? Do you believe God can deliver your spouse? If you do not believe in the power of God, stop pretending and deal with your unbelief first. Proverbs 18:2 says. *"Death and life are in the power of the tongue: and they that love it shall eat the fruit thereof."* Why do believers only believe this when it comes to spiritual things? I encourage you to eat the fruit of life and begin to speak life and resurrection power over you and your marriage. Speak death to the works of darkness and the bands of wickedness. Do not allow yourself to become addicted to the pain which can cause you to be blinded from the purpose of the pain. I am here to tell you there is purpose in your pain!

If you are the reader that is struggling with your flesh in remaining faithful to your spouse, I encourage you to first submit your flesh to God, for he is the God of all flesh! You have to make a decision to submit your flesh to God or submit your flesh to Satan and the works of the flesh. Do not let your flesh destroy your prophetic future and your marriage. You have to make the choice! If your choice is to submit to God, then seek deliverance quickly, and deal with your issues which have nothing to do with your spouse. Take that burden off your spouse and deal with you! Find a mentor and/or accountability partner; someone who is strong in the Lord and will hold you accountable. Someone who will stand in faith agreement with you that you can be faithful and honor your covenant. You can be delivered and set free! Remember heaven is backing you! Not only is heaven backing you, heaven is watching you and THERE IS NOTHING TOO HARD FOR GOD! God can do it in you and through you, if you let Him!

FINAL PRAYER

I decree and declare a shift over every person that has/is reading this book. A shift in your home, a shift in your finances, a shift in your deliverance, a shift in your marriage, a shift in your family. A super natural shift from glory to glory! I pray for a divine intervention and a divine encounter with the Holy One. Let every scale be removed from your spiritual eyes. Let every smoke screen be dismantled and let the Wind of Heaven blow upon each person, each marriage and/or each person that is preparing themselves for marriage. I call forth the resurrection power of Jesus Christ to resuscitate and bring back to life that marriage that Satan has tried to steal, kill, and destroy. I speak life, healing, and deliverance to have its perfect work in every marriage. I speak death to the covenant breaking spirit and death to every negative word, thought, or deed spoken over the marriages. I command the spirit of rebellion and disobedience to flee. I call the family unit back to the divine order of God and the original blueprint that was established from the foundation of the earth! May the clarion call to restore the family be released on earth as it is in heaven! Father, release your host of heavenly angels upon each person that has/is reading Damaged Goods to bring forth healing and restoration to their heart, mind, will, and emotions. Help them to know and believe in you on a far greater level than they have in the past. Destroy the root of family secrets and let every bloodline demon be exposed and expelled. Uproot the seeds of bitterness, unforgiveness, malice, and anger. And release your healing virtues over the hearts of your people. Release your angel of strength to assist each person during their process. Strength to endure, strength to trust you, strength to fight, strength to remain faithful to you, strength to not waiver, but to stand strong on your Word! For there is nothing too hard for You!

May your damaged goods become a beautiful love story! And it is SO!

JOURNAL

Your Thoughts & Notes From This Chapter

~ABOUT THE AUTHOR~

Shawney Tim is first a servant of the Most High God. She currently serves at the Center for Manifestation also known as Manifestation Worldwide, under the spiritual leadership of Apostle Mark T. Jones, Sr. and Prophetess Lisa Jones.

She humbly serves on the Prophetic Team, Bereavement Team and is the Ministry Lead of the Deliverance Team. She was ordained to the office of Prophet in 2016. She has a BA Degree in Christian Psychology and enjoys mentoring and counseling.

She is the loving wife of Reggie Tim, Jr. for 22 years. The mother of the anointed Prophetess Dacia Carter, who fuels her inspiration and stepmother of 3. She is also the proud grandmother to Jada Heavenly.

Shawney is available for conferences, workshops, and speaking engagements.

Visit us on:
www.shawneyltim.com

www.ingramcontent.com/pod-product-compliance
Lightning Source LLC
Chambersburg PA
CBHW071122090426
42736CB00012B/1983